A RAGE FOR OPERA

A

RAGE

FOR

OPERA

Its Anatomy as Drawn from Life

ROBERT LAWRENCE

Illustrated with photographs

DODD, MEAD & COMPANY
NEW YORK

ISBN 0-396-06319-5
Library of Congress Catalog Card Number: 70-145397
Printed in the United States of America
by The Cornwall Press, Inc., Cornwall, N. Y.

For Miša Petrović

Acknowledgment is gratefully given for help and advice in the assembling of photographic material to Mary Ellis Peltz of the Metropolitan Opera Archives; Gerald Fitzgerald of *Opera News;* Richard O'Harra, Columbia Artists Management; Dale Heapps, Hurok Attractions Inc.; Peter Gravina; and to the generosity of Roger Gross, Mary Hanlon, Lois Kirschenbaum, Thomas Lanier, Ruben de Saavedra, Richard Striker for the loan of items from their private collections. Two key photographs have been made available through the courtesy of *The New York Times* and of *OPERA* magazine.

—R.L.

CONTENTS

ILLUSTRATIONS

Following page 80

With Admiration

Birgit Nilsson as Turandot
Rosa Ponselle as Rachel
Kirsten Flagstad as Elisabeth

With Affection

Lotte Lehmann as the Marschallin
Maria Olszewska as Octavian
Maria Jeritza as Sieglinde
Giovanni Martinelli as Eléazar
Giuseppe De Luca as The Barber of Seville
Lawrence Tibbett as Simon Boccanegra
John Charles Thomas as Germont
Alexander Kipnis as Gurnemanz
Ljuba Welitsch as Salome
René Maison as Herod
Bidu Sayao as Violetta
Jennie Tourel as Adalgisa
Jussi Bjoerling as Gustaf III
    (*Un Ballo in Maschera*)
George London as Amonasro
Licia Albanese as Mimi
Cesare Siepi as Oroveso
Joan Sutherland as Donna Anna
Montserrat Caballé as Norma
Norman Treigle and Beverly Sills
    as Caesar and Cleopatra
Richard Tucker as Cavaradossi
Grace Bumbry as Lady Macbeth
Nicolai Ghiaurov as Philip II
Carlo Bergonzi as Manrico

With Esteem

Zinka Milanov as Aïda
Leonard Warren as Iago
Leontyne Price as Elvira (*Ernani*)

PROLOGUE

Irrational. Petty. Destructive. Such, in large part, is the private world surrounding opera—an ambient given over to preciousness, false pride, deceit. Here and there glow the lights of an ideal applied, a kindness administered. But for the most part this country is dark, the roads treacherous.

Revel in the lowering landscape? Share it with noisy fan-clubs, stiff-necked divas, conniving agents? Cheer the forward march of take-over tenors, the decaying repertoire set up for their star appearance?

One man's answer: *quand même* . . . all the same. Living opera does bear these blotches; yet one elects—for the art's inner qualities—to be near it always, shutting out the less agreeable surface sights and sounds.

Every step in this domain is made through personal preference. And any book on opera as a performing medium must spring from one man's taste—sobered, if you will, by a degree of leveling experience but still intensely, passionately subjective. And in such a vein I offer this compilation of operatic loves, hates, and one-night stands.

1

THE AUDIENCE

Deliver me from my warmest admirers.

(prayer attributed to the Unknown Diva)

YACKS, CLAQUES and ribbon salesmen with orgasms cali-
brated to high D did not always sit out front for opera.
But always is a long time and they've been there for most
of its history.

In the beginning, opera was played in Florentine palaces
before groups of *dilettanti*. These Renaissance aristocrats
speculated about the nature of Greek drama, which they
were trying to revive and embellish. Like the navigators not
long before them who, in seeking a passage to Cathay, discovered by chance a whole new world, these explorers in
their quest for antique theater—poetry, music and gesture,
the proper blending of one medium with another—were to
stumble upon modern opera.

Once music prevailed over its companions and the human
voice became all important, the new art headed from princely
quarters in the direction of the general public. The first

opera house was opened at Venice in 1637. Less than a hundred years later, opera had spread through western Europe, borne by touring Italian singers and maestri, some of whom also went on to the Americas.

No matter that opera moved from palace to theater. It preserved a regal bearing. Money and privilege followed in its wake. The baroque-inspired opera house created an architectural display of beautiful people, of polarization between boxes and pit, nobility versus mass, that was to remain the traditional design until several theaters of this type, blown up during World War II, had to be replaced by structures in tune with another age, different thinking.

Along with old-time rank, flaunting of wealth, indolence in the loges, gaming and ices in the anterooms, came the early squabbles of the buffs, founders of today's ribbonly-orgastic line. One can hear their voices across the centuries:

"But tonight's *castrato* is divine. . . ."

"Lunkhead! Next week you'll hear a good one."

"And the soprano . . . has she ever been surpassed?"

"By every door that squeaks. Have you no ears?"

Ill-sprung ardor can lead to bad manners, and these go back a long way among opera audiences. Cliques in London at the time of Handel went so far as to drive two celebrated prima donnas to a hair-pulling match onstage during a work tailored to their rival talents by the composer Buononcini. Egged on by a public eager for blood, they came close to shedding it. Music was not in the hearts of the public that night, nor could it have been dramatic art. The buffoons in the boxes, the barbarians in the pit were approaching opera as a feral game—a *corrida*—in which one of the participants must be slain or the heart at least be made to skip a beat.

Better to read about more perceptive listeners of long ago who welcomed the composer as well as the diva . . . audiences at Prague, Vienna, Paris in the act of hailing a live Rameau, Gluck, Mozart. Other creators in years to come were to share these public marks; but the later type of approval was too often shaped by fashion rather than love. For an account of audience taste at a leading Italian house in the 1820's, one turns to the pages of Stendhal, first-rate novelist but weather-vane critic, whose zeal for the operas of Rossini seems to have been fired less by grasp of their merits than by a passion for the social climate at La Scala where they were given in his time: boxes filled with beautiful women and elegantly attired officers, dashing visits from one anteroom to another at inter-mission or, if stage business were tedious, during the show.

In other countries too, vogue and creation were to inter-lock. Newly rich business men and their families, in the France of Louis-Philippe, attended the theater to see and be seen, solemnly paraded the length of the great foyers, their stiffness of dress and behavior matching the heavy grandeur of the opera houses and the sumptuous Meyerbeerian spec-tacles on stage; while in central Europe countless municipal theaters, adapted to folk opera and *bürgerlich* audiences, coexisted with the glittering repertoire of royal houses in Munich, Berlin and Vienna, and the austere Wagnerian syndrome at Bayreuth.

In the United States, from the advent of railroad barons to the outbreak of the Depression, opera was the province of the very rich. Society—and the struggle to enter its ranks by owning a box—prevailed. Powerful bankers, great con-tributors all, were able to command the engagement of the finest artists from abroad, sometimes importing composers as well (Puccini, Humperdinck, Granados). They shaped a standard of performance that had much to commend it; but the behavior out front, based on social snobbery, would not be in favor today. I recall how, many years ago on odd-Monday nights (the fashionable subscription series), at least half the Metropolitan's box-holders would delay entering the house until the first act was nearly over: private dinners preceding the show must not be hastened. These same groups thought it fashionable to leave early. They applauded sparingly, if at all; and the present Monday subscription, last vestige of top-hatted times, though stripped by now of late arrivals and early departures, still brings out the chilliest, least receptive among opera audiences. Ask the singers. They loathe performing on Monday nights.

No greater contrast to this Anglo-Saxon aloofness may be imagined than among certain volatile elements of the Latin public—resulting in just about the same disregard for opera as an art form. For myself, a centrist, the frigidity of a stuffed-shirt audience and the irresponsibility of aficionados run wild are equally alienating. Demonstrations have long been a way of life in the theaters of Italy, often tied to political goals. The Italians regard opera—because it was born in Florence, raised in Venice, armed in Naples, Rome and Milan—as their national strength. Instead of victorious admirals, conquering generals, they have had Rossini, Bellini, Donizetti. And in Verdi, who composed the operas of his youth while Italy still lay under the Austrian yoke (with libretti, despite the Hapsburg censorship, full of patriotic allusions), the militant side of the Italian spirit found a champion. Verdi's music, robust and fiery, came to symbolize freedom, unity. Later on, reaction was to spill over from pride in the works themselves to passion in the judgment of their performance.

Today there are many different kinds of public for opera in Italy. Touring companies play for support at the primitive level. Stove-hot emotion is their commodity, with structure, line, musical subtlety largely ignored. The traveling singers, when not trumpeting top tones and holding them at length, will indulge in a variety of "effects" that have small place in the drama: sobbing, weeping, caressing a phrase, playing with it, goosing it, thinning it from forte to purling pianissimo. Staging is rugged, orchestral playing rough, total impact one of slaphappy extroversion. And the provincial audience reacts as if at a sporting event. Cheering, it courts the vocal home-run.

One or two steps above this type of production is the more urbanized variety to be heard in the "second" theater, or *Politeama,* of most large Italian cities. The scenic crew is better organized, the orchestra a degree more precise, the singers better known. Yet the same knock-'em-down drag-'em-out approach prevails here as well—that burgeoning vulgarity described among cultivated men in Italy as *"Politeama* style." Audiences frequenting these theaters are outspoken, demanding a repeat (*bis!*) of solo numbers that please them, projecting at other times a brand of disapproval that can devastate the singer. Whistling and hissing may easily prevail, as well as applause. My thoughts go back toward the end of World War II, an evening in Florence at the Teatro Verdi (barracks-like "second" house), when a public of this type met its match on stage. Galiano Masini, colorful and reputedly semi-literate tenor, performing as Cavaradossi in *Tosca,* was in poor vocal form during the first two acts. His singing drew venomous shouts, scornful murmurs. And then in the final act came Cavaradossi's "E' lucevan le stelle," which he managed beautifully. The mood of his tormentors changed, melted. They clamored for a *bis*. Masini, ex-longshoreman from Livorno, stepped to the footlights, glared at his audience and said, "Up yours!"

It is quite a climb from the lowly *Politeama* to the level of the major Italian houses, especially La Scala (more deserving of renown today than in the time of Stendhal). Top-ranking orchestra, chorus and soloists, a wealth of musical rehearsals, staging and decor ingeniously and lavishly prepared, make for performances of exceptional quality. And one's pleasure is heightened by the splendor of the house, the elegance of the public. Not only in Milan but in Rome, Naples, Palermo and Venice are there theaters of majestic build. Turin and Genoa await the refurbishing of fine houses, one destroyed by fire, the other by wartime bombardment.

Yet no theater values can stay unchanged. Great as these houses are, today's opera-goer may find much about them that courts the anachronistic, including the audience. Indeed the fashionably dressed first-nighters at the Milan season of 1968-69 were pelted with eggs by youths calling for the democratization of opera.

The young men's protest was morally well taken: enough of snobbery in music; but aesthetically it touched on ground less certain. If a total stripping away of luxury out front should be imposed by fiat or the continued hurling of eggs, then opera itself might suffer in performance, for, let's face it, many of the works created for a nineteenth-century public based their final effect on dash and beauty in the auditorium as well as in the music. I have in mind the lustrous time of

Rossini, Bellini, Donizetti, when the relationship of a diva to her boutonnièred partisans was a very special thing, and the flamboyant epoch of Meyerbeer, the jewelled radiance in the house matching the brilliance of spectacle on stage. Deglamorize certain types of opera, and you're giving only half the show.

More real has been the alienation of modern Italian intellectuals from opera not as a social but a performing art. In that centuries-long gap from the instrumental age of Vivaldi, Corelli, Tartini, Geminiani to the opera-laden end of World War I (only Paganini happened to the local concert platform in between), music in Italy meant exclusively song. A revolt against this parochialism was begun during the 1920's by Respighi, Casella, Pizzetti and Malipiero, still writing for the theater but working outside it as well in symphonic and chamber media. And the young Italian *cognoscenti,* who had already come to despise vocal tricks, primitive posturing, overripe staging, were stirred by the appearance of new music other than song. They rebelled against traditional opera, turned away from it.

Yet their sons have been led back into the theater by singers . . . enlightened ones, not the sobbers, whiners or shouters. The new approach—as exemplified by the art of Maria Callas and other more recently emerged performers of Italian opera—has lain in grafting modern psychological awareness onto the older works, taking a new look at their characterization and musical style. Significantly, few of these artists can lay claim to great—even endearing—voices; but their taste, imagination and fire have drawn intellectuals once again into the opera house. The creative stage director too has won a response from this same generation: Luchino

Visconti, Giorgio Strehler, Franco Zeffirelli, Giorgio De Lullo—inventive in our time.

In short, audience conditions at the highest level in Italy could be optimum, reflecting the achievements on stage. But we come to the worm in the apple: the bigoted, intolerant opera buff, the self-appointed authority who attempts with strident voice and baneful manner to rule the house from his place inside it, to impose his special tastes on others. It is he who hurls scallions in contempt for the singer who displeases him, interrupts the opera with hisses, boos and catcalls. No less vile is this oaf's euphoric cousin, given to halting the music in its tracks with raucous bravos. Even the atmosphere at La Scala, potentially the best of possible worlds, is poisoned by extremists who, incapable of responding to opera as an art form and intent only on exhibitionist display, foul their own nest.

This hateful custom of the isolated listener functioning as judge, jury and executioner surges to massed limits, all dissenters joining forces, at the Teatro Reggio of Parma, the city where Toscanini was born. The Maestro's scorn for anything less than perfection is often invoked in the process; but these choleric buffs, so eager to show off, forget that the Toscanini tantrums erupted at rehearsal—a closed session—rather than performance. Dedication and professionalism kept him from acting otherwise. Not so with the town's public, which strikes terror to the hearts of all artists. Tenors have been replaced in action at the Teatro Reggio like pitchers at a baseball game. And the saying goes among singers in Italy that if one "passes Parma" (in other words, gets through without being struck out), one's reputation is

secure: indicating the total severity—one might say brutality—
with which this audience approaches opera.

I do not for a moment advocate complacency in the face
of poor performance. A bad job ought not to go rewarded.
It is the matter of public style, not principle, that stands in
question. Audiences of taste and ingenuity have proved that,
once the music has ended, there can be reputable ways of
signaling their displeasure. I recall one such demonstration
in Mexico—a disastrous *Trovatore* at which concerted public
action, cruel yet dignified, was hatched on the spot in answer
to bad singing. As the third-act curtain closed on the tenor's
"Di quella pira," miserably mangled, the audience—to a
man—joined in a spontaneous "SHHH!" There was no applause. The curtain never opened for the culprit to take his
bows.

One finds the same type of rejection, informed perhaps by
greater elegance, far to the Latin south in Buenos Aires. Unlike the natives of Parma, prone to murmur, bumble or shout
in token of how much they know about opera, the Argen-
tinians wear their learning gracefully. Inside the hushed and
breathless Teatro Colón, they lean forward in concentration.
If—when the music has ceased—they approve, it is with a roar.
Otherwise they are punishingly silent.

Only recently have I learned that this stony resistance to
bad performance may also be found in northern countries,
notably in Scotland. At a festival *Rigoletto* that I attended in
Edinburgh (1969), the Duke of Mantua's singing of "Parmi
veder le lagrime"—shoddy in the extreme—was followed not
by "SHHH!" nor in fact by any sound, but by a well-bred
sitting on hands enough to freeze the most insensitive tenor.

Not so in New York where audiences within the past

decade have abandoned discretion, developed their own style of aggressive ebullience. Bravos, boos, demonstrations during the act are "in"—a fanciful reconstruction of Golden Age fervor that has little to do with music but represents a kind of therapy whereby frustrations of daily life may be washed away. The shouters, concurrently with the artists on stage, are expressing themselves, giving their own performance. No matter that, among the public assembled, they are in an absurd minority. They interrupt, prevail, take over.

These are, however misguided, the idealists. I know of others. The arena spirit that has invaded the Metropolitan and held it captive is also in part the product of a few volatile, interracting forces: delegates from the record industry, whooping it up for the stars on their commercial label; impassioned ethnic groups; and strident teeny-boppers swayed by both other factions. I cannot, in the absence of full documentation, be more specific. But anyone with reasonably alert ears, time enough to spend around the opera house, and access to inner-circle talk will have detected the pattern.

We may dismiss from consideration the old-fashioned claque, whose heavy-handed applause and perfunctory shouts of approval have remained so obvious across the years as to be a give-away. Nor do we pause for the fan clubs of two decades ago with their throaty calls for certain Leonoras and Mimis. These are in retirement or elsewhere. I have reference, rather, to the yacks Trojan-horsed into carefully chosen and diversified locations throughout the theater, keeping their fingers on the pulse of the performance, giving it the gun when necessary. Most of these shouters may be distinguished, while working *en masse*, by their bizarre intonation of "Bravo!", less a sound than a grunt, a sandpapered football cheer. Of chief importance is their skill at stopping the show—literally—to milk applause for minutes on end. By results they gain, these worthies justify their keep; artistically it is another matter. The dignity of the opera house has been defiled, the performance made a patchwork of stops, shouts and starts.

The ethnic groups throw their caps into the air for any stars from the old country. National pride too often becomes chauvinism; chauvinism, frenzy. And if the artists in question belong on an important recording list, there is every chance of a double-header out front. On such nights, many of the uncommitted among us feel a dark anger bordering on violence. When will these knaves be silenced? When will the music go forward, the assertion of authority by management get under way?

Yet even these soirées in the theater do not reach the outer limits of audience behavior. That, in New York, is reserved for concert performances of opera. The aberrations here are more spectacular, an atmosphere of hieratic camp in command. Individual singers may be hailed on the spot as heroes or reviled as outcasts according to the audience's passing mood. Music is just the launching pad. We are back in Stendhal's La Scala of 1825, where fashion and caprice were determining artistic factors. Only here there is no real fashion, only a gaudy façade.

What to do? How to live inside opera and preserve one's love for it? A temporary solution, until after the intruders have been ousted: attend Wagner and Strauss "live" (they leave no chance for audience uproar during the musical flow). Enjoy everything else on records or tapes in the quiet of one's rooms.

THE REPERTOIRE

MY BEGINNINGS as an opera-lover date back to the days of Giulio Gatti-Casazza and those star-filled performances at the Metropolitan in the late 1920's when one could hear on successive nights Chaliapin, Ponselle, Pinza, Gigli, Rethberg, all in pristine form. Yet even then the glory of the singers impressed me less than some feats of repertoire that Gatti brought to pass. I remember a golden trio, one night after another, of *Boris Godounoff*, *Pelléas et Mélisande* and *Götterdämmerung*. Great artists were on hand to do them justice; but the point remains that these works were being given as part of a grand seasonal design. Repertoire came first; the stars, no matter how important, were considered later.

Obviously such operas could not have been mounted without adequate singers. (I say "adequate" because, in a pinch, the work must go on despite momentary gaps or inequalities in casting. Thus, until Lauritz Melchior's first New York Tristan, one was used to hearing the rôle attempted rather than sung. The Isolde, and the music, had to carry the occasion.) But somewhere inside that terrain reserved for capable artists, there are scores which no grand design, even the most high-minded, may bring off without a full celebrity. Revivals of *Armide, Semiramide, Otello, Louise* are unthinkable lacking the presence of a star who bears the needed vocal prowess or charisma.

Indeed one's last thought, unless he were a martinet stage director, would be the abolition of stars. Performances in which the cast functions strictly as a unit have small value if the singers are not first-class. The total, after all, cannot be greater than its individual parts. Such "ensemble" operas as *Don Giovanni, Così fan tutte, Das Rheingold, Don Carlo* call for distinguished artists in every leading role. The value of great singers cannot be minimized.

And yet, after these personalities have come and gone, it is the composer who remains outstanding in our particular world. The well-being of opera is linked to creation, basic repertoire. Whenever I read managerial quotes to the effect that we must repeat popular operas and avoid the unfamiliar in order to keep our houses open, I reach the conclusion it might be better—under the circumstances—to close them down. These theaters enjoy tax exemption for educational purposes, including, presumably, the diffusion of new ideas. Yet what of the educational can there be about still another *Tosca,* the tenors who hold on to "Vittoria! Vittoria!" until pried loose by applause, the clique-clack-yacks who demonstrate wildly for at least four minutes (an interminable break in the running time of a performance) when the soprano has finished her "Vissi d'arte?" This is not art in residence, it is the arena—or, rather, the abattoir.

Then what, if the reader is still with me and accepts my premise of the composer as paragon, should the repertoire contain? How ought it be planned? There are two ways of approaching the task. Inevitably, the large house will be concerned with chronology, the presentation of several different operatic styles and ages, including our own. For the smaller theater, local history and traditions, or sometimes bizarre and passing trends, work well. In this latter sense I am thinking of the repertoire for Brussels' Théâtre de la Monnaie—a venerable building with a modern outlook—for the season of 1969-70. No Puccini; one Mozart; one Wagner; two Verdi; one Strauss; *Dames at Sea* (the off-Broadway musical); Kurt Weill's *Mahagonny;* Auber's *La Muette de Portici,* whose inflammatory account of the Neapolitans' revolt against Spanish rule inspired a group of Belgian patriots, on leaving a performance of *La Muette* at this same Monnaie back in 1830, to fight in the streets of Brussels against Dutch hegemony; a smattering of French and Flemish opera; and, for the resident ballet, *Le Sacre du Printemps.* This is a repertoire reflecting individual (the manager's) taste rather than considered historical balance, but *what* taste! Bold, adventurous, successful.

A great international house, such as La Scala, the Vienna State, the Metropolitan, Covent Garden, Teatro Colón, has different responsibilities. Whim must give way to balance. And every period of opera in its special glory, charm or perversity deserves to be shown. This most certainly includes the Baroque, of which my own generation—save for a few influential scholars such as Paul Henry Lang, Winton Dean, Herbert Weinstock—remains wickedly ignorant. The American Handel revival, such as it is, has been spearheaded by younger men. As a musician culpable, with most others in his age-group, of having bypassed this master in the library, I have tried to bridge the gap in part by making his acquaintance on stage. Opportunities have not come often. There was *Hercules*—which, though technically not an opera,* has been described by Dr. Lang ** as "the greatest of Baroque music-dramas"—at La Scala during the late 1950's in a production with computerized staging and an ill-adapted though famous cast (Schwarzkopf, Barbieri, Corelli, Bastianini and Hines) that told me nothing. Some years later a musically fine though visually mannered *Giulio Cesare* at the New York City Opera opened the doors to Handel's presence, an experience reinforced shortly after that in a concert mounting by the same forces of *Semele* at the Caramoor Festival.

It would seem the duty of any leading house today, in the light of expanding musical tastes and knowledge, to mount Baroque opera with frequency, splendor, understanding, so that a whole new audience might experience something of its style and heart. Not only Handel; not Monteverdi alone among the early Italians; but all the great masters preceding Gluck, whose *Orfeo*—by an arbitrary arrangement—is said to mark the beginning of our standard repertoire. It is time, looking backward, to press ahead. The difficulties of presenting old music for the stage are many. Theatrical fires of early days ate into more than one master score, with reconstruction jobs devolving upon scholars of our time. Leading roles written for the *castrato,* then in vogue, have had to be reassigned with his passing. Several of the instruments in the orchestra of Monteverdi and his contemporaries are now

* Actually a secular oratorio, like his *Semele,* written for concert performance but closer to the theater.
** In "George Frideric Handel," W. W. Norton and Company, 1966.

obsolete. Thus practically no opera before *Alceste* and the two *Iphigenias* of Gluck may be given without some degree of alteration or rescoring. The field is open to musicologists of sensitivity—I propose they be assigned on regular duty to the major opera houses—to scholars of creative bent, to impresarios of vision, to recreate a part of the repertoire dimly perceived up till now and even more rarely produced.

And what of the Gluck operas themselves? We are used to *Orfeo* in the Berlioz edition of 1859, which combined most of Gluck's original * score with his later Paris version, and handed the rôle of the minstrel to a mezzo-soprano in tunic ** as a replacement for the *castrato* of bygone days. Among the other works, *Alceste* comes seldom and inadequately, its drama congealed by "classical" production, its song turned stiff and stilted. *Armide*—gorgeous, exotic, requiring not a stroke of revision or updating—has gone unheard on the American scene, except for an occasional student performance, since the era of Olive Fremstad. Both scores on the Iphigenia theme—*en Aulide, en Tauride*—have made the concert platform in our time but not the operatic stage. All in all, the modern view of this composer is a murky one, and sadly unjustified. On sitting through an *Orfeo* sung in oratorio style, danced and dressed like a ballet school annual, on listening to *Alceste* in the unadaptable throats of Wagnerian sopranos full of *Todesverkündigung*, critics who refuse to look beneath the surface proclaim Gluck as dated, lacking in profile. Non-professionals in the audience, alienated by what they are given to see, hear, and read the next day, have

---

* Vienna, 1762. The French premiere took place twelve years later.
** The celebrated Pauline Viardot-Garcìa.

come to share this view. And so the composer, victim of a Germanic 1925 revival style, has been written off by our intellectuals and, more sadly, by music-lovers in general as a never-was. Rehabilitation will come only when a producing team fresh from a successful Berlioz *Troyens* (which, after all, took the Gluck operas as a point of departure) has been assigned to an *Iphigénie,* an *Alceste.* Vocal tone, in such a case, will be clear, acting straightforward, orchestral quality spare and lithe, stage direction etched rather than painted. Above all, let's get Gluck out of central Europe. He once got out of there himself.

In the glow of today's Mozartean fire, it is hard to realize that two of his better known operas, *Don Giovanni* and *Le Nozze di Figaro,* have each been absent from the stage of the Metropolitan for twenty-two years, an unplanned but striking coincidence. *Don Giovanni* lay in abandon from 1908 to 1930, *Figaro* from 1918 to 1940: testimony to a changing repertoire, the unpredictable fortunes of works we consider operatic bedrock. Yet it seems unlikely that Mozart will ever again disappear from our leading house, even temporarily. Of all composers, he is most venerated by the confluence of generations in which we live. And a change in American performing style has been in part responsible. Vital, dramatic Mozart, not the impotent, mistaken tinkle-tinkle of the early 1900's, now shapes these operas' destinies, has made them living theater. . . . In Austria, needless to say, the composer's popularity came early, despite a cruel personal neglect. Bohemia, from the start, was receptive; Germany gave full acceptance later. There has always been a Mozart cult in

France, even though Berlioz was to cite what he regarded as anti-dramatic doodling in the closing measures of Donna Anna's "Non mi dir."

It has been in Italy that Mozart was and still is largely misunderstood. We know, for example, that *Così fan tutte,* first produced with success at La Scala in 1807, failed at a revival in 1814 and was not heard there again for 127 years. But *Così,* in any event, remains caviar almost everywhere. Italian taste collides more basically with the better known Mozart scores, for they are alien to a spirit that asks instant communication, prefers the sob to the sigh, the laugh to the smile. This lack of touch was brought dramatically to the attention of New York in the summer of 1968 when the visiting Rome Opera imported its production of *Figaro* as devised by the noted régisseur, Luchino Visconti. In a stated wish to break with what he described as the Viennese pastry shop tradition, Visconti imbued his *Figaro* with Milanese *verismo* of the 1890's,* blew on the revolutionary sparks in Beaumarchais' source comedy rather more than had Beaumarchais himself, until what came out—with great éclat—was a preview of *Andrea Chénier,* not bad, but not Mozart.

In England, through the well-suited theater at Glyndebourne, there have been performances not only of the standard Mozart operas but of that rarely given masterpiece, *Idomeneo.* Annual festivals at Salzburg, the composer's birthplace, profess to make—if not a specialty—at least a point of definitive Mozart productions. And yet, with or without the Salzburg rites, we are beyond the need of commemoration for this great composer. He is ours in daily life, together

* The type of stark realism—described as "a slice of life"—favored by Italian opera composers of that period.

with Verdi and Wagner one of the three mighty pillars in the operatic temple.

The pillars stand far apart. Within that broad space between Mozart and Verdi the opera-lover will find rare delights, the impresario his most slippery footing. Here, in this watershed of styles and motives, this cross-over from one century to the next, this transformation of opera from courtly medium to a launching pad for ethnic and political ideals, one of the few works that remain to us as standard is *Fidelio*. In the German-speaking countries it is always present, the keystone of their repertoire. Within our own precincts it lurks offstage half the time, waiting for the right dramatic soprano to make it animate. The soprano arrives, the triumph follows; and then disuse sets in again until the next trip. Perhaps it is the *singspiel*-type construction—spoken lines alternating with song—that alienates us, a public attuned to opera sung from one end to another. Thus have we kept under wraps the original dialogue version of *Carmen,* superior to the all-musicked revision (by another's hand) that has replaced it; and thus do we dabble, cutting and snipping lines here and there, with *The Magic Flute.* Whatever the reason for our lack of ease in the face of *Fidelio,* it does exist; and only a transcendent performance can sweep away the reservations we ourselves impose upon this masterpiece.

If so established a work as *Fidelio* has its difficulties, its years spent on and off the stage, the more specialized operas of this period put in a still rougher time. Would the *Medée* of Cherubini (in an Italian translation with recitatives added years later by a German *kapellmeister*) ever have regained the stage if not for the dramatic genius of a Maria Callas?

Since her assumption of the role, it has been taken in our time by Eileen Farrell, Magda Olivero, Leyla Gençer; but we may safely assume that after Callas no longer sings the music—which is now—this opera will once again fall into long-slumbering neglect. A similar fate has overtaken *La Vestale* of Spontini, once a great vehicle in revival for Rosa Ponselle, now gathering dust on the shelf (if we except a passing concert version of a few years back that featured Régine Crespin).

Like *Fidelio,* Weber's *Freischütz* stands at the heart of the German repertoire; but rarely does it take off on an international flight. Its folk feeling, its enchanting woodland flavor seem to lose in transplantation, coming through only when the performance is supreme. What of the other Weber masterpieces: *Oberon,* that problematical fairy tale, cut and revised whenever it reaches production; and the grandiose *Euryanthe,* alternating between supreme inspiration and awkward compromise—a work which, in the words of a great singer who has performed it, Elisabeth Rethberg, "neither lives nor dies"? Impresarios generally avoid these operas; and yet they can bring startling pleasure. I recall a revival of *Euryanthe* during the 1937 Salzburg festival as among the thrills of the season. Not only did the villainous duo for Eglantine and Lysiart (those forebears of Ortrud and Telramund) strike fire, but so—despite a few lapses—did the rest of the opera, with its chivalric panorama of the Middle Ages.

Most boxed in of all among the works in that wide Mozart-to-Verdi area are the once universally admired operas of Giacomo Meyerbeer. I have prepared and conducted much of this music: an activity I cite only as evidence of an approach that is first-hand, not theoretical, for with Meyerbeer, as with no other composer, one must beware of judgments expressed in the history books. An adequate biography in English, a perceptive analysis of his works in any language has still to be written. Almost any reference article now available—slanted through years of Wagner-induced hostility *—will deal grudgingly with the composer's orchestral skill, patronizingly with his musical invention, damningly with his taste, accusing him of selling out to the lowest bidder. Unlikely tales have been told of how, during rehearsals at the Paris Opéra, he would quiz the charwomen on their reactions to his latest work and make changes accordingly.

The truth, without preposterous embroidery, is that Meyerbeer aimed to please too widely; his major fault remains an eclecticism shaken off only at the most communicative moments. But to nail him relentlessly on the question of taste while overlooking similar breaches in others—Bellini's "Suoni la tromba" (*Puritani*), Puccini's "Vissi d'arte" (*Tosca*), "Ch'ella mi creda" (*La Fanciulla del West*)—is to weigh the scales grotesquely. If one listens receptively, he will hear the sound of the modern opera orchestra for the first time in Meyerbeer: the massed sonorities of the four bassoons, plangent murmur of the English horn, coruscation of the harps, 'cellos often playing darkly *above* the violas, trombones used not only for power but in softly menacing blocs as well. And in *Les Huguenots,* as the assassins brandish their swords, Meyerbeer's orchestra opens up in a fury that can make one's hair stand on end, trombones and piccolos rising on the same implacable pattern four octaves apart.

---

* Wagner, whose hatred of Meyerbeer—bigoted and irrational—has grown into popular legend, conducted an unending crusade against the man.

More important: this orchestral excitement is a mirror of the passions onstage. Meyerbeer's climaxes still rank high, but they need recreative power today. The love duet of Raoul and Valentine (*Les Huguenots*), the death beneath the mancanilla tree of Selika (*L'Africaine*), the unaccompanied trio of Robert, Alice and Bertram (*Robert le Diable*), are pages to be sung and played with extraordinary skill. Among the few remaining Meyerbeer traditions, his leading roles have become the domain of star singers only. Any less gifted—as at a disastrous concert performance of *Les Huguenots* not long ago in New York—will bring down the cause of the composer they are trying to serve.

The five-act grand opera pattern followed by Meyerbeer allows for a lot of sprawl; and what helps in modern performance is enlightened editing; cutting, tightening, passing over the lesser places, a process used with other composers from the same era. Whenever *Guillaume Tell* is heard in one of its rare revivals, one knows the editor's scissors have been at work—and not to Rossini's disadvantage. *Rienzi,* were it to be mounted today as Wagner's single attempt at old-style grand opera, would have to go through the same pruning process in order to survive. And with Meyerbeer almost every abridgement, respectfully taken, can work toward a credit balance. His major operas, smartly trimmed and well sung, might regain their place within our shrinking repertoire. Halévy too, in *La Juive,* still calls for attention. Some years ago, I made the mistake of reviving this work in concert form. It bored the audience, though not for the reasons adduced at the time. The opera remains strong theatrically; but the music takes its cue from the stage alone, reflects an allied rather than a primary interest. Some of it is excellent and, as part of history ignored, *La Juive*—with great singing-actors—could merit a fully staged replay, a fresh, spectacular look.

To judge from the current New York repertoire, one would imagine that Hector Berlioz had never written a note for the theater. Yet in London this master has arrived with a notable production of *Les Troyens* at Covent Garden in 1957, an infinitely finer one—the opera completely restudied and re-set—twelve years later, and a stunning *Benvenuto Cellini* in 1967. During the Berlioz centenary year of 1969, Covent Garden further took the remarkable step of dropping an annual Wagner *Ring* cycle and concentrating on the two Berlioz operas in its place. And in this same commemorative year, Sadler's Wells undertook a sensational and controversial mounting of *La Damnation de Faust:* a misstep, even if on a gallant path, for *La Damnation,* despite all past and present efforts to stage it, was conceived as a dramatic cantata (the structure tells us) and ought, for best effect, to remain in the concert hall, using the listener's fancy as magic lantern. *Les Troyens, Benvenuto Cellini* and the slender *Béatrice et Bénédict* are Berlioz's true operas, and the first of these ranks among the great of all time. Why, then, the delay in recognition at the "Met," why the long-standing barriers?

Another big French work neglected by our theaters is the *Hamlet* of Ambroise Thomas, due for large-scale revival when the winds of change blow through our halls. Detractors have made much of the ending, at variance with Shakespeare. Hamlet does not die. With Claudius slain, he ascends the throne—successor to his father. Yet only a man who chooses to ignore the text and bypass the music will take this ending for "happy." A burst of trumpets crushing rather than festive marks the curtain's fall. Hamlet, in the opera, *is doomed to live:* his final line, an agonized "My heart is in the tomb, alas, and I am King!"

The opera has stature. It also serves as a grand starring vehicle for baritone vis-à-vis lyric-coloratura (Ophelia, of the Mad Scene and many other moving pages). And the part of the Queen, sumptuously written for mezzo, suggests at times the impact of an Amneris. Yes, many jibes have come Thomas' way; but *Hamlet* stays an imposing work, eloquent and consistently dignified—more so than its contemporary from across the Alps, *La Gioconda,* which departs from the Victor Hugo drama on which it is based more wildly than does *Hamlet* from Shakespeare. Yet as a shameless fan of the super-colossal, I must own to admiring *Gioconda,* last of the old grand operas, prizing its Parisian-type dinosaur bones, expertly strung by that master paleontologist from Cremona, Amilcare Ponchielli. And there exists, by miracle, within the reconstructed skeleton a protoplasmic urge that organizes and propels such moments of genuine beauty as Enzo's "Cielo e mar," the concertato of the Cà d'Oro scene, most of the final act.

Fancy yourself at a concert-opera performance in Carnegie Hall. Imagine you are trapped in a nest of budding oafs doting on their favorite diva with as much tenderness as they had ripped without mercy into her adversary some four or five weeks previously, and you may understand, though perhaps not approve, of how a loathing for Bellini—the springboard for all this—may enter one's heart, make one overly hostile to the thin orchestral sound, sub-routine choral writing, pallid harmonic layout (save for those passing chromatics that are said to have charmed Chopin). What one cannot resist, of course, are the great vocal phrases, the rhythms on which they ride. I write not of *Norma,* that acknowledged and burnished masterpiece, but of the uphill, downdale *Puritani, Sonnambula, Pirata.* On the surging side, they bring intimations of genius. In descent, they are faded, formula-ridden. Too often in *bel canto* style, vocal refinements shape the expressive idea.

Turning to Rossini, one reacts with admiration and—less warmly—with a sense of distance, of a soft wall. This consummate musician made few attempts at personalized mood,* leaning instead with imposing success toward epic, semi-abstract states of feeling, as in the great rainbow chorus that ends *Guillaume Tell.* Even his celebrated humor was spaced rather than pointed, pattern as opposed to flash. The separate numbers are often superb; yet they seldom join in the sequential line, the thread of Ariadne, that is part of modern theater. As a result, no other composer—not even Weber or Meyerbeer—is today so often cut, transposed, rearranged in performance. The fault is largely that of impious hands laid on; but Rossini remains not entirely blameless. He is lacking in dramatic transitions and sometimes, as in the weak finale of the otherwise captivating *Le Comte Ory,* in climaxes. His instrumentation, especially in the later, Parisian period is formidable; the vocal line beguiling. Rossini was, above all, a professional, and on occasion—as in Mathilde's lovely aria, "Sombres forêts" from *Guillaume Tell*—more than that, a communicant with humanity. He has his champions, especially in Italy, where he enjoys something of a cult. Hardly a season passes at La Scala without the revival of an obscure

---

* Among the sparing exceptions: the entire, portentous last act of his *Otello.*

or neglected score. And this is as it should be. Rossini's music, in its elegant and uncompromising clarity, represents one great aspect of the complex Italian spirit.

Yet the thought occurs to me that, internationally, Donizetti will survive and flourish in a way denied to both his famous colleagues. They have become distinguished relics. He is still with us by reason of a vibrantly personal approach, melodies that soar, orchestral tone that colors specifically rather than abstractly, an advanced harmonic feel, ability to characterize strongly in whatever medium, lyrical, comic, or grand.

Like those around him, Donizetti sometimes fell into the trap of formula writing; but more often he would escape through bold, imaginative means. And on occasion he transcended his era, as in the melody "Verranno a te sull' aure," ending the first act of *Lucia di Lammermoor,* timeless and haunting, that goes to the roots of operatic song. He is a composer for today, and his lesser known works are being restudied not so much as outlets for diva display (although that too is possible) as for their basic riches.

The heartland of the repertoire is, of course, the domain of Giuseppe Verdi. He speaks to all men, and on all levels: an inevitability achieved only by the Bible and a few ageless bards. It is as if this music had always been there along with rocks and trees as part of the universal landscape. Its simplicity can appeal to the least tutored among listeners, its complexity reward the most exacting of scholars, its excitement get through to both. His works are the most durable in performance by any great composer. They may be done unsatisfactorily but never destroyed. Some protesting tune, some homely bit of action will rise up to save them. Produce a *Don Giovanni, Tristan, Pelléas* badly and it dies onstage. No so with *Rigoletto, Traviata, Trovatore.* Even when trounced, they bounce back again. This toughness of fiber may be part of their appeal.

Richard Wagner as polemicist never mentioned his rival Verdi by name. Was his scorn too great or his fear overwhelming? Whatever the motive, and we shall never know, his disciples were to break this silence years after his death. During the peak of post-Wagner adoration at the turn of this century when Meyerbeer's stock went up in flames, Verdi too got mildly scorched. It was alleged by fans of the Meister that Verdi's operas up to and including *Aida* had been only trial runs, preparations for the ultimate, Wagner-influenced *Otello* and *Falstaff.* This nonsense eventually blew away. The early operas, inventive and strong, had been no preparation but an end in themselves; and Verdi was his own man. Then in the decade after World War I a second attitude came into play, this time reverentially: the rediscovery by Franz Werfel and his Berlin-Vienna circle of the remarkable "experimental" operas: *Simon Boccanegra, Un Ballo in Maschera, La Forza del Destino, Don Carlo,* in which Verdi—trying for fresh communication even after the popular successes of mid-career—explored new musical, orchestral, dramatic techniques.

The public of our time has gone further than the "experimental" works, beyond the previously unfamiliar *Nabucco* into the terrain of *Luisa Miller* and—in Italian houses—*La Battaglia di Legnano, I Due Foscari, Stiffelio.* On the basis of hearings in depth via stage and discs it would seem there is no single opera by Verdi totally lacking in appeal. One or

two, such as *Ernani* or *Alzira,* may show him off form but
never at absolute zero. There are always redeeming pages.

He is not easy on performers. Several who swim easily in
Puccini have been known to battle the Verdian waves. Baritone and mezzo parts lie sternly high, tenor roles are marked
by long, breath-consuming melodies, often without orchestral
"cover," soprano assignments bring constant tests of range
and agility, felling those singers with heavy, inflexible voices.
Yet even with these built-in dangers, Verdi is in essence in-
destructible. The show moves forward (*"Tira avanti!"*) no
matter what the casualty: a compromise, in short, for productions on an ordinary level. The splendor of Verdi in top
performance, seldom revealed, is a mountain peak as seen
through parting clouds.

If one could reach into the operatic past and touch what
has meant most to him, I should lay hold of those wonderful
years at the old Metropolitan that brought the annual Wagner cycle: not only the works themselves but the special
atmosphere, blending the solemn and the festive, the superlative singing.

We were innocent in those days of anything but the most
conventional staging, relying instead on the eloquence of
certain great solo artists. And then it came, after World War
II: the new concept out of Bayreuth, an approach that
stripped away all surface decor, molded the visual element
in Wagner to the enigma of the poem, the riddle of the
music. Spears, helmets, trees, other paraphernalia from the
literal past were to vanish.

So be it. I am undisturbed if that transforming moment
when the door of Hunding's forest hut flies open to reveal

Siegmund and Sieglinde bathed in moonlight is suggested
not by swinging canvas but a radiant change in the night
sky. It needs hardly be argued that the historical picture-book
approach represents only one of several ways in which Wagner's works might be mounted.

I *am* disturbed, though, when voice and orchestra in this
same act are filed in the opera house to a whisper or blown
on discs into sonic inflation. Fortunately such liberties prove
less than fatal to the *Ring*. Another famous maestro, another
studio producer will reverse the trend before too much time
has gone by. We are in an age when Wagnerian values, on
the whole, manage to stay in balance through wide pendulum
swings. And he who loves the music may remain reasonably
happy, as do I, except in one agonizing area—the fading, or
attrition, of *Tannhäuser*.

Stray bits of truth are ranged in synthetic patterns to account for this opera's decline: too much of the action is old-
fashioned and grandiose, the title rôle is cruelly written, it
has a high tessitura that can finish off most dramatic tenors.
But whenever any great opera house undertakes *Otello*—in
which the name part is also notoriously hard, albeit on different grounds—does it not seek and find the requisite tenor?
And do not *Aida, Gioconda* and other operatic staples contain
a good deal that is theatrically ponderous? The cause for the
decline of *Tannhäuser* does not really lie in attributes. It is
wedged, rather, among the attitudes and prejudices of our
impresarios, our recording executives, all uptight over critical
myths out of Germany.

Before considering these myths, a quick look at the performing history of *Tannhäuser*. The first version came to
light at Dresden in 1845, a time when Wagner was not yet

equipped poetically or technically to fill the cave of Venus with the color and allure that would be his in those later days leading to *Tristan*. The overture begins with piety: the well known Pilgrims' motif passes sensuously to life inside the Venusberg, then swings back on itself to a brassy return of the evangelist tune—militant virtue knocking the spots out of vice. Applause. Curtain up. Brief and sketchy bacchanale followed by a scene for Venus and Tannhäuser in which the goddess, alternately wooing and reproaching, suggests a hectoring housewife. The phrases are angular, ungrateful.

Sixteen years later, when Wagner revised the opera for production in Paris, he was at the height of his powers. Not only did he expand the bacchanale into the most sumptuous of orgies, bowing to Parisian taste for a full-scale dance episode. Also, in response to a compulsion of his own, he rewrote the entire first scene for Tannhäuser and the goddess, lavishing on Venus some of the most glorious music ever to come from his pen. As it emerged, the revised role may be sung either by full dramatic soprano or by high mezzo—a significant overlapping, for most of the part lies in the rich central portion of a darkly tinted voice.

It is not generally realized that Wagner retouched six episodes in all for the Paris *Tannhäuser,* of which the Venus scene remains the longest and most celebrated. That lacerating run for massed violins at the end of Act Two, when the hero, overwhelmed with guilt, kisses the hem of Elisabeth's gown, then rushes from the hall, is new. It does not appear in the Dresden version. So are various other elaborations (and occasional tightenings) that have improved the opera. And of course the pompous return of the Pilgrims' motif at the end of the overture has been dropped. The Venusberg music of the orchestral introduction fuses—via a dramatic upsweep of the curtain while it is in progress—with the bacchanale on-stage. This last refinement, a postlude to the French production (in which the old-style overture had been retained), was introduced at the Vienna State Opera in 1875. Today the Paris (-Vienna) version, in its rare hearings, is all·of a piece—overture melting into the dance.

I have written "rare hearings"; and yet the Paris edition was the one on which today's middle-aged New Yorkers grew up. During the 1930's and early '40's, this superb music was constantly in use at the Metropolitan. We enjoyed a soprano Venus with Kappel and Marjorie Lawrence, mezzo with Branzell and Olszewska, all these artists bringing us the sound of Wagner's creative maturity. And now it is over. Word has gotten around (those myths out of Germany) that a conflict in styles is involved, that the heady, chromatically involved Paris Venus cannot be squared away with the chaste, harmonically guileless Dresden Elisabeth, and so the whole of the 1845 original is trotted out—and rejected by a generation that wonders what we ever heard in this opera.

The impresarios and the record executives! Can they not understand that Wagner *wished* his Venus and Elisabeth, enchantress and saint, to exist on irreconcilable levels, that, in his Paris version, he deliberately set two contrasting worlds side by side? The antagonism of provincial German theaters, unequipped on technical grounds to stage the later bacchanale, has—under the slogan of "unified style"—passed to the larger ones and, reinforced by pseudo-scholarly gobbledygook, affected even the great international houses. I can recall hearing the Paris Venus only once on a first-class stage in recent years: Vienna. And almost unbelievably, except for

an obsolete recording of the great duo for Venus and Tannhäuser (as sung by Ruth Jost-Arden and Sigismund Pilinsky
at the Bayreuth festival of 1930), *there is no version of this
scene on discs.*

The end was reached at a Metropolitan Opera revival of
the late '60's when Birgit Nilsson, in what was announced
as a feat, sang both Elisabeth and the Dresden Venus * at the
same performance (quite feasible, since they never appear
onstage together). Had she gone into action with the Paris
Venus, we might have experienced the kind of thrill reserved
for a great artist's doubling, if that were physically possible,
in one evening as Aida and Amneris: surging contrasts of
tone, phrasing, passions. We heard, instead, Aida and a minor
colleague, the Priestess. Just a bit later, *Tannhäuser* sank.
Purists to the contrary, one would hardly think of offering
Verdi's *Boccanegra* minus its Council Chamber scene—which
belongs to a version of twenty-four years later—or *Don Carlo*
without the wonderfully retouched confrontation between
Elisabetta and Eboli. This is operatic common sense. Why
should it not be used in presenting Wagner?

All my life in music, first moderately and then ardently, I
have been drawn to French opera. It is not a domain of giant
composers, excepting—in less than a handful of works—
Berlioz and Debussy. It owns no constant masters on the scale
of Mozart, Verdi, Wagner. Yet it strikes a unique balance
between Italian vocal hegemony and German orchestral insistence. Doubters will demand, remembering larger sounds
in other places: are there any real climaxes? And I should
answer: plenty—though never inflated. The muscular and

* She recorded them subsequently.

sensitive are here inseparable partners. It is well, while approaching this repertoire, not to think in purely musical terms. In its wizardry of pacing, disdain for the obvious, elegance as a performing medium, French opera breathes totality of approach, stresses theater itself as the end-all.

And yet, though full of admiration for the sponsoring brand, I dislike its two best known products, *Faust* and *Carmen,* which radiate to excess the one quality apt to spoil French opera even for its fans: an overpowering sweetness suggesting the smell of cheap perfume. This scent permeates, in varying degrees, several other French works: all of *Lakmé,* where it takes on an oriental cockroach-killer aroma; much of *Les Pêcheurs de Perles,* the same fragrance more deftly disguised; parts of *Les Contes d'Hoffmann,* in which the spell of the opera itself offsets the pervading musk.

Once recognized as a factor, this element need not, unless too strongly concentrated, mar enjoyment. In the case of the great masterpieces, such as *Pelléas et Mélisande, Les Troyens,* its absence is complete. And yet though demonstrably on hand in Gounod's *Roméo et Juliette,* it detracts not at all from the grace and pathos of that charming work. Perfume in opera, minimally applied, should work no final harm, but when blended with ecclesiastical body-odor, the damage can be enormous; and in *Faust* this sweetness cum smugness poses a problem of basic acceptance. Everything is banal: the facile hero, strutting Devil, purling tunes—well, *almost* everything. In the hands of a sterling performer, Marguerite comes alive and moves us, be it in the garden, church or prison. Gounod at best was a composer of lyrical attainment. But the lack in *Faust* of lean dramatic strength, subtly shifting color strikes me as un-Gallic; and this is a lack, though easily borne in another repertoire, which may not be tolerated in the French.

And *Carmen?* Even in the spoken-dialogue version (Bizet's own), minus those recitatives added by Ernest Guiraud after the composer's death, we have the marshmallow Micaela, the one-dimensional figure of Morales (Zuniga, his fellow officer, is more sharply drawn); the bullfighter himself, musically square; the undifferentiated stand-up quartet of the smugglers and their girls. One agrees that the last act from beginning to end remains a work of genius. But what about the rest? This was an opera set up by Nietzsche as an antidote to the Wagnerism he detested, free of pomposity, the fairest example of clear-eyed Mediterranean outlook; and yet, except for that justly renowned last act and a few earlier scenes marked by the presence of Don José (the one superbly handled character), *Carmen* lacks inner tension. Surface brilliance, yes; and a few tragic bull's eyes, such as the wonderful motive associated with fate. But we are considering principles rather than details, organic drama as expressed through music. More than one critic has written of *Carmen*—rather naively, it seems to me—that he has never seen or heard a really satisfying performance by any singer in the name part. This because, always excepting that miraculous final act, the lady isn't there. Her part remains a mirage, a strongly scented Spanish-gypsy try. The tunes are well spun; Bizet's scoring is adroit. Yet one expects more sustained theater from French opera, and has received it from composers less "safe" and officially commended.

To name one: Jules Massenet, a lyric talent walking in the shadows cast by epic masters. The overlay of elegance in his music does not blunt its directness any more than traditional cadences in the Mozart operas (Berlioz to the contrary) can weaken their dramatic truth. With him one finds the comfort of the accessible, the Petit Trianon rather than the Parthenon. After the heaven-storming scores of Verdi and Wagner, what opera buff might not welcome so relaxing a prospect? Despite a deceptive simplicity, Massenet has conjured up—vocally, orchestrally, atmospherically—operas of widely ranging mood. To type him by the glitter of his masterpiece, *Manon,* would be inaccurate. In *Werther* and *Le Jongleur de Notre Dame,* he dispensed with elaborate decor, spectacular ballet, coming up with deeply moving simplicity. And there are other facets to his gift for the theater. The one-act battle opera, *La Navarraise,* hurtles hotly toward a realism not otherwise associated with this composer. *Thaïs,* given two strong performers as the monk and the courtesan, spells out imaginatively, even if doused with that inevitable perfume, a study in moral conflict. As music-lover and performer, I revel in the operas of Massenet, in their intimacy, their diversity, their instantaneous charm. If this be superficiality, I shall gladly plead guilty. No other opera composer has returned in our time from among the supposedly dated with such luminosity and conviction.

Other milestones in the French repertoire: Charpentier's *Louise,* a work with the city of Paris as heroine. Using a device reminiscent of *Tannhäuser, Maria Stuarda, Les Huguenots,* in which the prima donna does not appear until the rise of the second-act curtain, Charpentier also waits before introducing his diva—this time not of flesh and blood but of the spirit, a great metropolis—glimpsed for the first time at the foot of Montmartre, after an opening act played inside a workingman's apartment. The role of Louise herself, though secondary to the city in which she lives, is a strong one. Does she not—intent on escaping from a smothering environment at home, on dwelling among the free souls of Montmartre—anticipate today's rebellious youth? And Charpentier's music, inventive now as when first composed, exudes the beguiling and often malodorous fragrance of the corner brasserie.

Less accessible, but vital in its own right, is Paul Dukas' aristocratic retelling of the Bluebeard legend in *Ariane et Barbe-Bleue.* The orchestral score glows and flames; the voices soar; and yet the drama is interior, which is not surprising, for *Ariane,* like the shadowy *Pelléas,* is based upon a play by Maeterlinck. For those whose operatic beginnings date back—as do my own—to the decade before World War II, one of the stirring memories is that of Germaine Lubin singing this music at the Paris Opéra. She brought power and clarity, made it overwhelmingly impassioned. And last among the milestones comes Poulenc's *Dialogues des Carmelites,* of which the final scene—the procession of the Carmelite nuns to the guillotine, singing their "Salve Regina," the voices one after another silenced by the fall of the invisible blade—remains one of the most shattering in opera. These are, for me, the high points of French musical theater in our century, peaks too often left unexplored.

If one's resistance rises at all to the Slavic repertoire, it is on a minor point, having to do with performance: the tendency of almost every basso taking leading roles in these operas to have listened excessively and slavishly to recordings by the great Feodor Chaliapin, to submerge his own singing style in favor of one that came naturally to a man apart but sounds hollow and contrived in the throats of others.*

This single point aside—and a surface one, at that—how can the dedicated opera-goer respond less than unreservedly to a repertoire in which music and theater are combined with an immediacy that strikes to the quick? The door to this Slavic treasure-house is opened, by consensus, through a knowledge of *Boris Godounoff*, one of the three or four top masterpieces in any language. As happens with every work touched by the sublime, battles still rage about *Boris*. Moussorgsky's score has undergone retouching by various editors, chief among them Nikolai Rimsky-Korsakoff, and a determined group of critics has called for a return to the composer's pristine thoughts and sonorities. A great idea, but I wonder how many of the critics who write so learnedly about Moussorgsky's instrumentation have caught the sound in performance. It is almost never heard by reason of technical drawbacks that have drawn helping revisions not only from Rimsky-Korsakoff, whose version has become standard, but Dmitri Shostakovich and Karol Rathaus. The issue may be resolved in time by grafting most of Rimsky's expert orchestration onto the original, filling in his arbitrary cuts with instrumentation by others, scrapping his remaining editorial changes. Whatever the outcome, the miracle of *Boris* remains its power to characterize individually and collectively, to weave ruler, conspirator, noble, peasant, holy, debased, into an epic tapestry rivaling in scope any devised by Berlioz, Verdi or Wagner.

Boris is the gateway to Russian opera, yet what of the land-

* Exception is hereby registered in favor of two artists who, in interpreting *Boris Godounoff*, have emerged with their own sound: George London and Cesare Siepi. Most singers make the music unremittingly thick, indirect, funereal—a parody, rather than a true rendering of the Chaliapin approach.

marks beyond? Moussorgsky's *Khovantschina* (also edited by
Rimsky); the luminous world of Rimsky himself—*Sadko, The
Snow Maiden, The Invisible City of Kitezh.* His *Golden
Cockerel* has survived sporadic horseplay by reason of an
elegance that cannot be downed. Yet even here the Russian
repertoire only begins. Glinka, Dargomyzski remain to be
explored. As for Borodin, we shall have some day a gorgeously
mounted, wisely edited *Prince Igor,* at present nursing a
critical black eye through inadequate local performance. And
the operas of Tchaikovsky—not only *Onegin* and *Pique
Dame,* but *Mazeppa* as well (Vladimir Horowitz, an authoritative buff, has great fondness for the last of these)—will be
done by major artists rather than the utility singers who now
serve them in the West.

If the great classics of Russian opera may be termed
neglected, then outstanding contemporary works are ignored,
except by such forward-looking companies as the New York
City Opera and the group at Santa Fe. Shostakovich's
Katerina Ismailova (recently come to us in definitive form via
a film version from the Soviet Union) and *The Nose;*
Prokofieff's *Love of Three Oranges,* which everyone knows
but few have heard in representative performance; his tragic
masterpiece, *The Flaming Angel,* and his farce, *Betrothal in
a Monastery,* are played only rarely on our stages.

The Flaming Angel has, to a degree, invited this bypassing,
for it is a vehicle in the same sense as *Medée, Norma, Elektra,*
demanding a soprano of almost superhuman vocal gifts and
theatrical sensibility. And so a New York presentation of a
few seasons back, despite the noble intention of bringing
the work forward, ended by doing it a disservice in the absence of a genuine star. Renata, the disturbed one, around

whom plot and music center, projects at the beginning a breathless confusion that strips away in progress to reveal the tigress, the demon beneath; yet this evil must be felt from the start. Like a juggler, the performer is constantly balancing musical elements against the dramatic, reconciling the vocally strenuous (especially in her twenty-minute aria, one of the longest on record) with the visually bizarre. A Callas in her prime might have done justice to this extraordinary role; a Rysanek, in the gifted and neurotic mold of her Senta, might still do the job. And then, in the presence of a gifted interpreter, we could enjoy—if that is the word for so devastating a work—the only Gothic opera of our time, a horror tale told by Prokofieff with an intensity and imagination that make it, for me, the most exciting music theater after *Elektra*.

Just as Strauss could turn from his one-act thriller to the farcical *Rosenkavalier,* so was Prokofieff able to leap from the darkness and terror of *The Flaming Angel* to the radiance and hilarity of *Betrothal in a Monastery,* a comedy that would grace any repertoire. Since good English versions of both these works are available, there is no need for grappling with them in the mother tongue, understood by so few among us. The translations are here. Where are the operas themselves?

And what of the world of Czech theater music, those tantalizing glimpses, via recordings or live visits by the Prague National Opera, of the riches beyond? Bedřich Smetana is moving, in our West-of-Vienna orbit, from audience focus on his lovely but genre-bound *Bartered Bride* to interest in the epic *Dalibor* and curiosity about *The Kiss*. As for Dvořák— discs of his music for the stage, current for several years now, reveal an uneven grasp of the medium but at its finest, as in the last act of *Rusalka,* a grand operatic brush stroke. In the matter of Leoš Janáček, I leave a description of his strengths to those who know them at first hand. I have followed only two of the works—*Jenufa* and *The Makropoulos Affair*—in live, professional performance. Of the fact they are durable, imaginative, exciting there can be no doubt. And also transplantable. Reports have come of successful productions—*Katya Kabanova, The Sly Little Vixen, House of the Dead*—on stages in London, Berlin, Milan. The first two have also cropped up as student mountings in New York; the third, professionally, on American television (NET). But there has been no Janácek at the Metropolitan (save for a *Jenufa* by the resident company back in the early 1920's, and the same piece given there again by the Hamburg Opera on a recent *gastspiel*). Similarly none at the New York City Opera until the landmark triumph in 1970 * of *The Makropoulos Affair,* following by two seasons a presentation of the work in San Francisco.

Oddities—where *do* they belong? Falla's *La Vida Breve:* Spanish in color but French in texture, its audience appeal international. Ginastera's *Don Rodrigo:* mod Meyerbeer—his *Bomarzo* starker in outlook—both works to be respected rather than loved. Stravinsky's *The Rake's Progress:* venerated by the Igorophiles—to my mind largely sterile, the triumph of manner *per se.*

One tires of those slick, unperceptive and generally inaccurate couplings of composers' names to be found in

---

* An edition that made an international star of Maralin Niska as Emilia Marty, the 342 year-old central figure. The resourceful staging by Frank Corsaro, the luminous conducting by Gabor Otvös will long be remembered.

musical journalese: Bach and Handel, Bruckner and Mahler, Verdi and Puccini. Such combinations are part of the syndrome about dual headlights, double-breasted suits, clasped hands on graveyard statuary. And of all these forced pairings, I find the Verdi-Puccini hardest to take. Aside from the fact that both men set Italian texts to music, there is hardly anything between them in creative cross-over. Verdi was stark, Puccini lush. Verdi worked in epic dimensions; Puccini was the genre painter. Every artist, one is aware, must be judged by the way he performs within his given medium. Only the amateur critic will confuse grandeur with superiority, consign intimacy to second place.

And so I pen this screed to Puccini not on the basis of size but taste. With the exception of *La Bohème,* an authentic, bitter-sweet masterpiece, and of much effective music (the book not withstanding) from *La Fanciulla del West,* the Puccini repertoire, in its hit-parade, middle-class cachet, stands a few steps aesthetically above *The Merry Widow.* The melodies are often appealing, the instrumentation skilful, the sense of pacing masterly. But is pacing alone to be confused with overall theater? Can tunefulness supplant ideas?

A key to Puccini's dramatic values may be found in his admiration for the work of David Belasco, one of the most successful—and hollow—among American theatrical figures of the early 1900's. In their treatment of heroines, the two men converged. Examine almost any of the Puccini divas from Manon Lescaut to Liù and you will find a continued dwelling on pathetic generalities, the same exaltation of self-pity (exception: the vindictive Princess Turandot). Only one of these women comes through with real, as opposed to manipulated, conviction: Giorgietta in *Il Tabarro*—dark, disturbed, believable. Cio-Cio-San keeps returning to a single attitude: the militantly fragile. Tosca, more volatile in part (for she is a creation of Sardou, not Belasco), still gets lost in a vale of sentimentality. Was ever music-hall ballad more maudlin than her "Vissi d'arte"?

Turandot, its vengeful princess aside, begins with enormous promise: uncompromising dissonances, weird orchestral sound. A violent, blood-stained Orient is evoked. Yet no sooner, after the rise of the curtain, does the unknown Prince find his father in the streets of Peking than this tone-picture gives way to the usual Puccini sob-line, as though the composer were bent on demonstrating (*vide* Marco Polo) that noodles first came to Italy from China.

We are dealing with a gifted man; and I should be disingenuous in not responding to his finer pages: the second-act love duet from *Manon Lescaut,* perhaps his most sensuous moment; all of *Bohème,* except Musetta's waltz song; much of the moody *Tabarro;* the "Te Deum" and remaining music given to Scarpia in *Tosca;* Jack Rance's monologue and, later, the poker game that brings down the second-act curtain of *La Fanciulla;* the warm-hearted quartet in *La Rondine;* and the big first-act choruses from *Turandot.* This makes, I believe, for a considerable total; and there can be no doubt that Puccini pleases a large public. My feeling about his works is purely personal. It is not their sound that turns me off so much as the facile, show-biz aesthetic behind them, and their endless, conveyor-belt reappearance in our opera houses, taking time and effort away from other scores, less familiar, that deserve powerfully to be heard.

Puccini represents, of course, Italian *verismo in excelsis.* My own preference runs to the red-blooded Umberto

Giordano, and his *Andrea Chénier,* a work of remarkable strength. In this tale of the French Revolution, the characters blaze, the music rings with passion. Why, then, should the same composer's *Fedora,* which too rides in on glowing sound, seem so dated today? The answer: a libretto of the silent movie type, a diva sporting pearls and a feather fan, high society intrigue, with all the fixings, in Czarist St. Petersburg, Paris, the Bernese Oberland. Yet the score itself has sumptuous moments. And I should commend to anyone in search of a comedy-opera Giordano's *Madame Sans-Gêne,* musically sophisticated, theatrically deft, which has been revived with good success in Italy.

As for those famous veristic twins, Leoncavallo's *Pagliacci* remains in better shape than most critics have predicted, its orchestral and dramatic expertise still to be admired, while Mascagni's *Cavalleria Rusticana,* with the exception of the superb duets involving Santuzza, is coming apart at the seams. And what of Mascagni's little comedy, *L'Amico Fritz?* Charming and vibrant on discs, self-consciously pastoral in the theater. At any rate, a departure from the outhouse realism of *Cavalleria.*

With so much talk of *verismo* in the air, one comes with surprise upon a different branch of Italian opera springing from the *Mefistofele* of Boito, and running with somewhat diffused intensity through the music of Catalani, Cilea, Montemezzi, Respighi, Pizzetti—sometimes languid, often eclectic, and once in a while genuinely vibrant. This is the more polished side of the repertoire but not necessarily, except in the case of Boito, the more imaginative. After a recent revival of *Mefistofele* at the New York City Opera, thousands of words were written about the opera's magnificence, its parity with the masterpieces. It seems to me the emotion of meeting with a major work too long absent from the scene, of attending a strong performance may, in this instance, have topped objective judgment. Yes, *Mefistofele* is unique. The Prologue remains without parallel in the annals of opera— somewhat to the detriment of the remainder of the work, which is swamped by so overwhelming a start. Garden and prison scenes still exert a spell, as does Easter Sunday outside the city gates; but the Witches' Round and ladies' seminary-type Classical Sabbath (Sir Arthur Sullivan appropriated one of the tunes from this number and burlesqued it in *Princess Ida*) now seem definitely old-fashioned. It is good to have *Mefistofele* back. One is struck by the bold approach, theatrical daring—but cannot close an ear to fluctuating values in the music.

And today in Italy? Rejecting the plush Respighi tradition, Luigi Dallapiccola has struck forward in terse, concentrated scores nearer in point of view to Arnold Schoenberg. Using such disparate stories as *Il Prigioniero,* rooted in the Spanish Inquisition, and *Volo di Notte,* set at a contemporary airport, and clothing them both in sound as sparing as it is eloquent, Dallapicolla has brought the Italian lyric theater— formerly so exuberant even when restrained—into new channels of poetic discipline. Of Luigi Nono, aside from his gimmicky *L'Intoleranza,* it is too early to speak. But all options, including mixed media, must stay open. Without a choice of new outlets, opera in our time is up against the wall.

The two Richards, Wagner and Strauss, stand infinitely closer than Verdi and Puccini. Naming them together has a dynastic ring, for certain works of Strauss, notably *Elektra* and *Die Frau ohne Schatten,* have brought to a climax the whole Wagnerian system with its symphonic approach to the opera orchestra, elaborate use of leading motives, expansion of the vocal range. This is not to suggest that Strauss surpassed—or equaled—Wagner as creator. My thought has to do, rather, with his handling of Wagnerian *technique,* in which the later Richard proved himself more royalist than the King.

On the surface of things, the post-Wagnerian world ought have been vast and populous. Yet aside from Strauss—and ultimately Alban Berg—central Europeans of this century writing for the operatic stage have turned out few significant scores. Engelbert Humperdinck, Hans Pfitzner, Ferruccio Busoni,* Eugen d'Albert * commanded briefly. Of the major composers, Gustav Mahler, renowned for his conducting of opera, was never to create one; Hugo Wolf, triumphant in his songs, made only one attempt—unsuccessful—at the theater; and Arnold Schoenberg's few ventures in this direction have proved largely doctrinaire. The field was left almost entirely to Strauss; and he made the most of his chance.

One's feelings in regard to Strauss might be likened to reverence for a great statesman coupled with chagrin at his burping in public—for Strauss, despite prevailing grandeur, had a disturbingly ordinary touch. How, for example, to reconcile that pedestrian brass tune for Jochanaan with the sensitive tone-painting in so much else of *Salome;* explain the Viennese waltz that keeps trailing Chrysothemis in *Elektra;* accept the harmony-trio clichés of Naiad, Dryad and Echo in *Ariadne auf Naxos;* put a good face on that wretched

---

* Born and raised elsewhere, but attracted to the Berlin scene: Busoni, of mixed Italian and German blood, was educated south of the Alps; d'Albert, of Belgian ancestry, grew up in Scotland.

jingle sung by the unborn children toward the close of *Die Frau ohne Schatten?* The answer would seem to lie in Strauss' power to transcend limitations of taste, draw the listener along unresisting. Thus, *Elektra* as the theater piece of the century—opera that leaps forward, burns of itself, enkindles others.

In *Der Rosenkavalier,* the work that followed, Strauss had a popular success; yet today's buff might spend happy years without missing its overweight comedy, excessive length. There are, to be sure, gratifications: that capital portrait of the Marschallin von Werdenberg—well dressed, well loved, a grande dame born to take suffering in her stride; the soaring duo of the silver rose for Octavian and Sophie; the closing trio . . . but the work is uneven—much of it musically a wasteland—and often gross. From the advent of the Composer in *Ariadne auf Naxos* to the appearance of the Countess in his final opera, *Capriccio,* Strauss was to spin a finer texture. Yet I see no point in the taking of sides, as is often done, about Straussian chronology, bearing down on the fiction that everything after *Ariadne* is either heaven or hell, according to one's persuasion. Sometimes it can be both: scrawny pages in the otherwise attractive *Arabella;* stolid ones in the generally imaginative *Frau ohne Schatten.* It makes no difference, really, whether the opera under discussion is early or late Strauss. Only one question must be answered: does it convince?

Berg's *Wozzeck* and *Lulu* were still considered far out as recently as twenty years ago, not in the German-speaking world, of course, but in France, Italy, England, the United States—and now they are "in." To discuss them today at length, especially *Wozzeck,* would be the equivalent of making learned table talk about *Tristan*. It has all been said before. Whatever the techniques that went into the writing of *Wozzeck:* abstract musical forms underlying the individual scenes, alternation of singing and song-speech (from Schoenberg), the twelve-tone basis on which most—but definitely not all—of the work is built, these are matters belonging inside the composer's laboratory rather than out, are of no moment alongside the unique stir aroused by this opera in performance. Long after researchers have stopped discussing the materials of *Wozzeck,* shattered listeners will be talking about Berg's ability to make the nerves quiver. *Lulu,* through the composer's early death, has come to us in unfinished form which poses severe problems in production; the musical speech is harsher, less accessible than in *Wozzeck;* but the score, in sound and action, is so much of our time, its psychological turmoil so relevant as to overcome all drawbacks.

Where has German opera gone from there? Along the Hindemith road, where one meets a masterpiece, *Mathis der Maler,* damned by many critics with the faintest of praise: the usual bit about nobility of purpose but inflexibility of pacing, plenty of intellect but little heart. For myself, the sound of *Mathis* is vital, the dramatic interest unflagging. What could not the Metropolitan, with proper casting, accomplish with such a work!

Then from Hindemith past Carl Orff and his monolithic operas to Hans Werner Henze, a composer performed throughout Europe and much of the United States: *Boulevard Solitude, Elegy for Young Lovers, The Young Lord, The Bassarids,* yet unrepresented in New York by a single work, save for a student performance of *Elegy.* Whatever the cause of this exclusion, just or unjust, we remain without scores that are international property. Their vogue may be shallow—but opera-goers would prefer to judge for themselves.

Which brings us to the English-speaking repertoire and the strongest work in any language since *Wozzeck:* Benjamin Britten's *Peter Grimes*—a splendid opera, its only flaw the passive, sexless heroine, Ellen Orford, her relationship with Grimes lacking in clarity and, ultimately, in truth. Still this bit of slack is minor alongside Britten's uncanny ability to catch the changing light and the tragic feel of his fishing village in their every variation. Almost equally valid, though of different density and texture, his *Turn of the Screw.* Repeated hearings of *Grimes* bring renewed pleasure; returns to *The Rape of Lucretia,* ennui and impatience with the precious libretto, Britten's almost too stylish handling of it. *Billy Budd,* on television and in concert (unstaged up till now in New York), has left an impression of the composer at near-best; *A Midsummer Night's Dream,* at his most mannered, with a few moments to compensate in final flight. One longs to hear the coronation opera, *Gloriana.* And one takes or leaves, according to his temperament (I leave), the three miniature monkish operas by Britten to be performed in churchly surroundings. Malcolm Williamson? Sir Michael Tippett? Their works have not yet come to us in depth. Richard Rodney Bennett's *The Mines of Sulphur,* as revealed in a student performance at the Juilliard, gave evidence of a man conversant with musical theater, its needs and its effects. Local writeups were lukewarm, the reviewers cautious. Unnecessarily, I thought.

America is the Rome of its day, great on absorbing and

emulating, short on the creative process. There has been, to be sure, no lack of trying; and a few moderately successful works have emerged: *The Ballad of Baby Doe* (Douglas Moore), *Regina* (Marc Blitzstein), *Susanna* (Carlisle Floyd), *The Mother of Us All* (Virgil Thomson), *Vanessa* (Samuel Barber), along with a formidable Menotti repertoire. Growth and development continue. Of all the decisions taken by Rudolf Bing during his reign at the Metropolitan, easily the most valiant was his commissioning of an American opera for the opening of the new house. Old hacks, professional and amateur, who can see and hear no further than *Aida*, cackled with rage when the choice of Samuel Barber's *Antony and Cleopatra* was announced, and later with glee when the opera failed so dismally. They had opposed, almost to the death, anything new; and, in the midst of their gloating over the fiasco, did not realize that Barber's opera had bit the dust *because it was not new enough.* The composer, a reputable musician with fine scores to his credit, had attempted the heroic mold, traditional grand opera, a style uncongenial to his intimate, somewhat retiring talent. It is to the credit of Bing and the Metropolitan that they were willing to take their chances, eager to consecrate the new house with a score born in this country. Success and failure were relative. It was a concept that mattered—the idea of opening a freshly built theater with a freshly created work.

Barber worked big in *Antony and Cleopatra;* Gian-Carlo Menotti has gone in another direction, more in tune with trends of the time he helped to shape. With *The Medium,* Menotti's most imaginative work, came the small orchestra—tailored, not cut down—giving the effect of a large one. Technical demands on the individual players (and in this he differed from the approach of Richard Strauss in *his* chamber group for *Ariadne auf Naxos*) are not severe; the orchestra men might easily be members of a workshop ensemble. Nor do the voice parts, though boldly written, lie beyond the capabilities of singers who bear no startling gifts. In short, the operas of Menotti are geared not to occasional and problematical production in a few large houses, but to constant, efficient and profitable mountings in small theaters and university auditoriums across the country. Since Menotti is his own librettist (and stage director), the works have notable unity of style. I admire the man so greatly as a theatrical force, as impresario (one has only to examine the programs year after year of his Spoleto festival to note the cool, challenging choices) that I regret being less drawn to his music. How so sophisticated a mind should have turned out the simplistic *Consul, Amahl and the Night Visitors, Saint of Bleeker Street,* is a puzzle not easily resolved.

A note for the future: it is possible that from our "straight" musicals—*Porgy and Bess, West Side Story*—there may develop, as happened in France with the opéra-comique, a complex and absorbing art form. I should love to see it, for these are spontaneous works, preferable to the stilted operas turned out on commission year after year with American foundation funds. If there were justice in the world, Mozart should still be alive and healthier than most of the travelers on that foundation gravy train.

THE SINGERS

FROM THE BEGINNING, the central stream of opera has been song. No matter what type of sonority—honeyed, guttural, florid, spare, expansive, straitened—it is the vocal art that dominates.

There has never been a serious break in the centuries-old love affair between opera and singing. True, the styles and principles revolving *around* that union have changed and are even now in transition. But the human voice itself, sole unifying bond in an art so tantalizingly complex, keeps to its path as an expressive force.

The ways of expressivity in operatic sound are many: the symmetry of a Handel; austerity of a Gluck; introspection (fronted by elegance) of a Mozart; chivalric dash of a Weber; liquidity of a Bellini; sinew of a Verdi; sweep of Wagner and Strauss; ruggedness of Moussorgsky; charm of Massenet; hothouse bloom of Puccini; disorientation of Alban Berg—all, despite enormous variations of style and color, are as one in the throats of those divinely endowed individuals whom at their best we hail as artists.

It is my belief that any singer with intelligence and flexibility should rise above specialized divisions of opera, be adaptable in all, come off with distinction in many. Happily there are more such performers at hand today than one had dared hope with widely ranging skills, enlightened preparation, international viewpoints. And yet the bad old traditions continue to thrive, those deeply rooted vulgarisms that masquerade as national styles. There is no reason, basically, for Italian performers to sob, Germans to force, French to pinch. Good singing transcends local habits, much as proper speech rises above regional dialects.

Genuine national differences—real, not aped—are welcome. They bring to a top vocal group the same diversity and contrast as do diverse schools of instrumental playing to a cosmopolitan orchestra: Russian string tone, French winds, German brasses, acoustically varied, blending to form a greater whole. Homogeneity of sound at dead center is no asset either in symphony or in opera. Fusion is the better aim. But such an approach brings new responsibilities, and in opera an artist of standing will have mastered many idioms beyond his own, have managed to couple balance and poise with expressivity at all levels.

In this respect, take almost any recording by Enrico Caruso. Granted, in advance, the glory of tone, dynamism of performance. Beyond that, seldom noted, lie the stylistic awareness of Caruso, his rhythmical impeccability, his freedom from those excesses—the smear, the cry, recklessly applied— that have so often brought forth, in the case of other tenors, the reproachful adjective "Italianate." Admittedly, for us raised in an Anglo-Saxon culture (I refer not to stock but mores) there can be nothing more embarrassing in the theater, no moment more disaffecting than that of hearing a grown man burst into sobs: a symbol of self-indulgence totally at odds with our outlook. There is no question here of *machismo* but rather the dignity of the human condition. And it remains part of Caruso's greatness that when he *does* sob—as on his famous disc of "Vesti la giubba"—the agony is so formidable, so right that it cuts across traditional lines, immemorial differences in custom, reaches out and shatters us. On the other hand, attempts by a Gigli to exploit this sob, "milk" it, make it part of a warehouse stock must, at least in our climate, lead to revulsion. Parochialism has set in, international communication vanished.

The Italians are not alone in self-limiting trends. Among the French, and especially their singers of today, a tendency to ram climaxes at the top has impaired the beauty and authority of a once distinguished art. Too many Russian sopranos (always excepting the superb Vishnevskaya) go strident and "white" above the staff. More than one German baritone leans toward the precious; and Scandinavian Brünnhildes, even among the famous, will chip at a high-lying phrase, detaching instead of binding, producing a chill effect. Desirable standards for judgment in our time would come from the singing of a de los Angeles, Ludwig, Gedda— the color and sound of homeland retained, but adapted to international tastes.

And I have been judging, man and boy, for over forty years. Styles have changed during that period, generally for the better. Singers today have greater respect for the music, resort less to showy effects, aim for an almost instrumental simplicity. While the chest tone, for example—that sensuous, dusky mode of producing the female voice at low altitudes— still takes root in the opera house, it is no longer used indiscriminately, belted by the ladies with an almost baritonal insistence. And only the most conceited or ignorant among male singers will hold on to resounding high notes without dramatic reason. Wilful display, except by provincial performers, is going by the boards. Most of today's leading artists seek, before going into performance, to be "motivated," to understand in depth the work's psychological needs, match them with every facet of their talents. Though practiced only now on a large scale, this approach is not new. Ezio Pinza was responding to it regularly when my generation started attending opera. So were Lucrezia Bori, Gertrude Kappel, Karin Branzell, Friedrich Schorr.

If any one artist seemed to have been favored by the gods, it was Pinza. The voice had no need of that process known as "placement." It was naturally produced, on any dynamic level at the will of the singer. The color was inherently dark and voluptuous, but in answer to shifting styles could be altered to the spacious and noble. Pinza sang most often in that veiled, caressing super-legato favored by Italian bassos, obscuring the forward, more brilliant quality which I know lay within his scope as well. That last "I know" is based on striking memories of the Pinza Oroveso in *Norma,* when— addressing the Druids, at the rise of the curtain, as their priest ("Ite sul colle")—he chose to lift the veil, project his voice on the clearest of beams. Just why Pinza should have reserved this transfigured tone for the opening of *Norma* remains a mystery in my book. Perhaps the texture of the music itself impelled that gleaming sound, or, more likely, the artist's instinct had tapped the right sonority.

Yet instinct is perhaps too vague a word in regard to Pinza. One would do better with "perception," for here was a thinking man. I have written of an artist favored by the gods, which signifies not only looks but flair, not only acting but musicality, not only voice but brains. It is said he read music with difficulty, had to be coached beyond the time given the average singer. If so, one is staggered at the labor that must have been involved, for the Pinza repertoire was almost all-inclusive, omitting only contemporary opera. His Mozart, Bellini, Donizetti, Verdi, Wagner, Gounod, Charpentier, Debussy were all etched with scrupulous care. And never, as I recall, did he allow himself a moment's exaggeration, lead the audience on, contend for its applause. Those readers who heard Pinza toward the end of his career in still another medium, musical comedy, will remember his dignity in *South Pacific,* the straight line of a performer who mastered the popular idiom, never coaxed it.

He was the hero of my youth, and Gertrude Kappel the heroine. I do not pretend that their gifts existed in like dimensions. She was not beautiful as Pinza was handsome, nor did she have his all-out theatrical flair. The voice too, though innately of the most exquisite texture, did not always answer to her wishes. In short, the gods had not lavished everything. And yet Kappel at her best, with that luminous sound in full working order, brought to the tuned-in listener a special psyche-to-psyche communication (all the more remarkable for not being consciously projected) that lay beyond even the most striking achievement of Pinza or any other singer of the time. Maria Callas, years later, was to possess this quality to a degree; but her effectiveness was blunted, for me, by self-flagellation rather than self-surrender, by an instrument that wrestled with minimal demands of vocal acceptability. With Kappel it was different. Except for her off-nights (caused, I believe, by some passing turmoil rather than vocal deficiency), this artist transformed word into tone with a musical subtlety, dramatic insight I have heard approached only once—presently, by Christa Ludwig. The conviction that came from within made Kappel beautiful on stage; the complete rendering of herself caused the voice to take on, in exalted moments, an added dimension. Above all, the range and complexity of vocal color were extraordinary. I recall another Wagner soprano of the time—the admirable and glowing Frida Leider—who sang more evenly than Kappel; and a famous colleague with a larger natural voice, Kirsten Flagstad; but neither reached out so unerringly to touch the nerve endings of him who would respond.

I had imagined myself, in recent years, as victim of a self-deluding fraud, a swollen memory, for Kappel made few recordings, and none among them suggests even remotely the voice and performing eloquence I treasured. Then—quite recently—there was issued in a collector's edition certain off-the-air excerpts from *Götterdämmerung* taken during a Vienna State Opera performance of 1933, and the beloved voice came through as I had remembered: warm, vibrant, giving. On the taped surface of that scene between Brünnhilde and her sister, Waltraute, a maze of static—scraping noises, blistering interference. Above it rose the Kappel sonority: "Denn selig aus ihm leuchtet mir Siegfried's Liebe!", pristine, recognizable for a few overwhelming moments as the sound of long ago.

Although Kappel as an artist radiated intelligence, she was primarily intuitive. Deeply rooted drives within her united word and tone came out of no planned synthesis. It was different with another idol of my youth, Lucrezia Bori, whose achievements seem, in retrospect, to have been governed by complete awareness. Not that she was ever cold or mechanical. The passion generated by Bori in the church scene of *Manon* as—unlike all singers of the part today—she sank to the stage on her knees and, in her ball gown, crawled its full width toward Des Grieux, must remain with anyone who saw and heard her. Her charm, distinction and pathos in so many other lyric roles marked a milestone in one's listening experience. This was, in contrast to Kappel's, an art minutely controlled and, for that, perhaps a shade less affecting. The Mélisande, for example, belonged always to this world rather than to another. But Bori's special qualities— her winsomeness, vivacity and, above all, the most patrician of tastes—made her irresistible in certain pages of Verdi, Puccini, Donizetti, Thomas, Massenet. The voice gives little evidence on records of how it traveled in the theater. One had to *see* Bori, combine sight and sound in one glorious collage. There was a cutting edge to the tone, a timbre related more nearly to oboe than flute, that gave excessive point to *dolce* moments but brought infinite brilliance in the climaxes. As to the handling of this voice, elegance and sensitivity always prevailed.

These were the singing-actors with whom I was most deeply involved. Others, too, exerted their appeal: Branzell and Schorr, Frida Leider and Maria Olszewska, Lotte Lehmann, Alexander Kipnis, Lawrence Tibbett, Michael Bohnen when exaggeration did not claim him. The singers I cherished were those who fused word and tone, tone and action. Inevitably, in doing so, they made certain vocal sacrifices. Beauty of sound had, on occasion, to go by the board in favor of dramatic effect. And yet there were artists at this time, persuasive actors too, whose outlook—primarily vocal—brought enormous joy. Rosa Ponselle of the noble voice sang a poised, authoritative Norma, excelled in Verdi beyond all others; Elisabeth Rethberg reigned, in a wider selection of operas, with a radiance lovably her own; John Charles Thomas brought a security and splendor rare among baritones then and now. We had, too, a unique "personality" soprano, Maria Jeritza, holdover from an earlier, golden-slipper age, who gave many striking performances; and an Italian tenor of high integrity, Giovanni Martinelli. No catalogue is here intended, only a string of outstanding memories, to which distinguished singing by Giuseppe De Luca and Richard Bonelli might be appended.

I happened in on all this during the latter days of Gatti-Casazza, that watershed era at the Metropolitan between the death of Caruso and the advent of Kirsten Flagstad, too late to have heard Farrar and Garden in the theater, too neglectful to have caught Chaliapin in his final years. It was a period characterized by bad orchestral playing, shoddy staging, but wonderfully imaginative singing—most of it on an intimate and lyrical scale.

The crossover came in 1935: the passing of Gatti-Casazza from the managerial scene, Flagstad's concurrent debut and the emergence of the big sound. Clarion sonority had made its mark a few seasons before that in the Wagner tenor section, or, to be more precise, through one member of it—

Lauritz Melchior. Though slack with rhythms and often rudimentary in acting, Melchior combined such sumptuousness of tone with expressive penetration that even now his Tristan and Tannhäuser remain unrivalled. In team with this artist, Flagstad raised the vocal standard of Wagner performances to thrilling heights. The power, security and ease of her singing (except for a curiously thinnned out, non-vibrant top) have not been equaled in my time; the quality of the voice itself, in the abstract, was hauntingly beautiful. Yet it was a quality that rarely changed with the mood of the drama; and since this is a jaundiced chronicle, I must admit to standing in the outer circle of her admirers. The impact of that marvelous voice in Brünnhilde's oath on the spear could not help but affect one; the precision of pitch, musicality of phrasing in Isolde's second-act love music were superb, but I felt no probing command comparable to that of Leider, no mastery of nuance as with Kappel. One night at the prewar Paris Opéra I was to encounter other shining aspects of acting and song in the French dramatic soprano, Germaine Lubin, plus a physical beauty that was unique; but they proved a flash along the way. Lubin, scheduled for an Isolde, Sieglinde, Kundry, Alceste in New York, never reached here owing to the outbreak of hostilities.

Edward Johnson, successor to Gatti, did manage before the height of battle to make some notable importations: Marjorie Lawrence by way of the Paris Opéra; Jennie Tourel from the Opéra-Comique; Bidu Sayão from Brazil; Licia Albanese, Alessio De Paolis and Salvatore Baccaloni from Italy; Zinka Milanov from Zagreb; Jussi Bjoerling from Stockholm; Alexander Sved from Budapest; Lily Djanel from Brussels—excellent artists all, received with varying degrees of welcome. We were also given John Brownlee of Australia; Martial Singher of France; and, in a brief flurry of brilliance just before the war, three outstanding Italians who were unable to return: Maria Caniglia, then a young artist developing her Tosca and Aida; Mafalda Favero, lyric soprano, one of the finest Mimis I have known; and Galliano Masini, a crude but stimulating tenor.

Layers of Wagnerian clouds seem to stand between Marjorie Lawrence and my memories of her earliest performances. Impressions sharpened, took shape during her second season here. Everything she did had vigor, musicality, an athletic drive best exemplified in her *Siegfried* Brünnhilde, quite the most exciting I have heard from anyone. I recall, as well, a first-rate Sieglinde, more lithe and passionate than the usual run. Above all—and this recollection is very clear, coming as it did after Lawrence's tragic bout with polio in which she emerged the moral victor—she was the definitive Paris Venus of our time, a role which she sang, seated, with a gorgeous range of tonal coloring.

Sved, with that wonderful, gamey baritone, never entirely came up to the expectations we all held for him; Tourel, bursting on New York with an overwhelming Mignon, established an enduring place for herself in both opera and concert. Djanel, the finest Salome of my experience after Welitsch, and Singher, both artists in the dramatic French tradition, had measured success as vocalists.

Of all these singers, the years have most enhanced the reputation of Bjoerling, a tenor of prime quality. His appeal—in the class of Ponselle, Rethberg, John Charles Thomas —lay in beauty of song. This is not to say his work onstage lacked vigor. It was, on the contrary, firm, energetic, but wanting in final communication. Only once did I see his powers realized on every level: an inspired Don Carlo that put him for that single evening in the handful of top singing-actors.

Sayão and Albanese, sopranos with small voices but each a splendid performer, were like two sides of the same coin: Sayão projecting a chiseled, elegant type of art informed, however, by passion; Albanese keyed to a larger design, more dynamic, and sometimes—from the point of vocal conservation—too exuberant. Both women had to rely on slender resources in coping with the opera orchestras of Puccini and Massenet; but they won, proving that well focused tone, backed by dramatic accent, can cut through any curtain of sound if the odds are not too persistently great.

With Alessio De Paolis, the Metropolitan acquired a *comprimario* capable of weaving the smallest character bits into the grand operatic design. He surpassed more than one leading tenor of the time through a dominating sense of opera as theater, a minute command of the player's art. And in John Brownlee, singing principal baritone roles, one recognized a similar respect for theatrical values—a polished artist, but rather too well bred for best effect onstage. No such reticence hampered Baccaloni, the famous comic basso, in both major and secondary roles, wonderful whenever he did not work too hard for laughs. One looks back with admiration at the refinement of his Mozart, the gusto of his Verdi and Rossini.

As for Milanov, her qualities were those of a superior vocalist. Many opera-goers of long standing swear by the memory of her *pianissimo,* her ravishing *mezza-voce,* and up to this point one stays in their company. Her musicianship, too, commanded respect. It was as an interpreter that I found Milanov less than strong, with fantasy in short supply. Only a single rôle, Gioconda, seems to have engaged her sensibilities at top level. In other frames of reference she brought distinguished singing, routine theatrical presence.

And yet this artist towered above most of her contemporaries. One soprano, alternating with Milanov in Verdi rôles, used so many different kinds of production (purling *pianissimi*, upholstered chest tones, plangent *fortes*) that the more Rabelaisian among her listeners declared she sang through every hole in her body. Then there was the tenor, Kurt Baum, whose acting ticked off historic moments of pre-camp camp. The voice was solid, the theatrical instincts fallible.

Brighter aspects of this time included the brief but impressive blaze of Dusolina Giannini, the best Santuzza of my experience, and of Gina Cigna, an exciting Aida; the first-rate artistry of René Maison as Herod, Loge, Florestan, Walther von Stolzing; the warmth of Bruna Castagna in a galaxy of mezzo-soprano roles; the charm of Jarmila Novotna as Cherubino and Manon.

As I look back on the Johnson era, it was often a shambles: choristers in badly fitting wigs and the wrong shoes, a drifting quality of ballet, the retention of certain solo singers through what must have been, at the least, debatable choice. In trying to gratify everyone, Johnson ended by pleasing few. And yet, for one noble resolve—successfully carried through—he deserved full marks. Faced with the drying up, during those war years, of European sources for his casts, he developed the American singer. Grace Moore, though a holdover from the Gatti regime, came into her limited but exhilarating own under Johnson as did, in lesser degree, still another Gatti alumna, Gladys Swarthout. Risë Stevens, Dorothy Kirsten, Eleanor Steber, Helen Traubel, Regina Resnik, Jan Peerce, Robert Merrill, Richard Tucker, Leonard Warren were all products of the Johnson era, some of them going on to international fame.

Stevens offered a winning Octavian and Cherubino, a lovely Mignon, and a Carmen—accepted as standard at the time—that I could not take seriously. Self-conscious theatrical vice got in the way of vocal virtues, set up another stone in that cemetery for unsuccessful Carmens, many of them quite convincing at other assignments.

Most beautiful of the Johnson voices belonged to Helen Traubel, who sang with poise and radiance. Top notes were not always responsive, but this did little to spoil the basic splendor. Her sound in Wagner came out big, without forcing—yet could thin to a melting *pianissimo*. Traubel's one real problem lay in a lack of expertise on stage. She came late to the theatrical world, having spent a large part of her career as concert artist, and never acquired the ease of movement, mobility of face and gesture that marked the pre-Flagstad sopranos at their best. Passing from the scene too early, she left little in the way of dramatic memory but much to have aroused one's appreciation of a sumptuous organ sensitively employed.

Richard Tucker, a New Yorker more fervently Italian by temperament than the most outspoken Neapolitan *scugnizzo,* has made his mark through ringing tone, superior musicianship, deepening artistic growth, while his brother-in-law, Jan Peerce, inclines toward a more intimate, patrician style. Both men, so different as natures and yet alike in their affection for Latin repertoire, have covered most of the lyric and *spinto* roles with distinction. Of this same native New York group, Leonard Warren—who began his career at the Metropolitan with a warm baritone of great size—turned inward to an almost priestly style, his former glow giving way to a subdued, meditative sound. The care with which he prepared all roles, the authority of his style could draw only admiration; but his grasp of the stage was something else again. I did not find him an accomplished actor. Something too deliberate, ritualistic got in his way. And yet the presence was forceful, the dignity high. He was an artist of class. With Warren's younger contemporary, Robert Merrill, the voice has stayed bright and forward, the timbre attractive without fail. But this exceptional baritone has brought not quite enough to his acting—nor, indeed, to all his singing—to celebrate the gifts innately his. One writes more critically of Merrill than of other first-line performers because his endowments are so striking. He has never, it is true, misused them. An all-pervading earnestness and, on occasion (as in *Don Carlo*), eloquence have marked his work. But he has still to marshal those talents, those spurts of performing brilliance into a sustained artistic pattern.

And, alas, for one who did—Eleanor Steber—there came a career that ended prematurely, latter-day inequalities covering the glory of her prime. For those who might be skeptical of the Steber preeminence, I urge a playing of recordings and tapes of this voice in its finest years (with special attention to Metropolitan Opera broadcast material). She was not a singing-actress so much as, in the tradition of Elisabeth Rethberg, a sterling vocalist of widely ranging styles and repertoires. Mozart, Beethoven, Verdi, Puccini, Strauss, Berg are among the composers she served with crystalline quality, virtuoso command, impeccable musical taste. She was gracious on stage and, early in her career, a real beauty. Whatever the reasons for a deterioration that came too soon, I recall her as a top artist, one of the beacons in those Johnson years.

Dorothy Kirsten, once Steber's rival in *Traviata* and the Puccini parts, has—conversely—kept growing. Not so much with the voice which, flexible and well preserved, has settled into a familiar format, but through developing insights into the theatrical side of her art.

Starting from this same era, Regina Resnik, first as soprano and latterly as mezzo, has injected such skill and drive into all of her work—with success even as Klytemnestra, a part demanding elaborate and weighty vocal powers—that I might only wish to be more in tune with her achievements. I do not find the sound inviting. Yet she is incontestably a front-line artist at a time when opulent voices of the Branzell-Olszewska-Castagna type seem no longer available for the big mezzo roles. In their place, Resnick brings her own credentials: versatility, professionalism, an enormous intelligence.

There were others: Martha Lipton, a lyrical Brangaene; Blanche Thebom, stylish in Mozart, angular in Verdi and Wagner; Jean Madeira, who sang Carmen well and mugged it badly; Jerome Hines, stately and sonorous. They came out from under the Johnson wing and went on to important assignments. Variable in cross section—but artists of worth.

The ending of the war brought an exciting resumption of European imports, among them the Italian mezzo-sopranos Fedora Barbieri and Cloe Elmo; no fewer than three leading Italian tenors: Ferruccio Tagliavini, Giuseppe Di Stefano,

Cesare Valletti; and, most notably, the flaming Bulgarian soprano, Ljuba Welitsch. All of them, cursed with the blight of brief career that overtook imported singers of that period, were destined for a short run on these shores; yet at their best they gave enormous color to the performances in which they took part. Both mezzos, excellent artists, succumbed to the forcing that seemed endemic to Italian operatic circles in the late 1940's. So did Tagliavini, a good "pro" with a certain theatrical flair. He pooped; whereas Di Stefano, a young tenor at the time, never quite grew up. The voice, so long as the bloom lasted, compensated for a slapdash lack of preparation. Later on, this fault became more apparent; the reputation shrank. Inherently warm, dramatically ardent, Di Stefano with his first-class vocal equipment should have stayed at the top. His failure to do so, in the face of a formidable talent, is to be regretted.

At this point, a meditation on Italian tenors. Vocal adversity seems to be their best friend. Those not endowed with a resplendent *forte,* a caressing *mezza-voce,* must turn inward, strengthen what resources they possess with intelligence, musicality, adroitness. Caruso stood above this division; he had everything. But in general the tenor who convinces stylistically will most likely be a bit short on vocal plush. Valletti was a case in point. Elegance and schooling gave him most of what was needed. Yet even he knuckled under to the blight that hit so many Europeans with careers dating back to the '40's: a premature failure of the machinery. Did this arise from a desire to sing too "big," too intensively? Only a voice teacher (and I am not one) might fruitfully speculate on the cause; we know the results as tragic.

Returning to the cultivated versus intuitive Italian tenor,

one meets Giovanni Martinelli, who with a relatively un-
beautiful and often pinched dramatic voice carved out for
himself a career based on expressivity, masterly phrasing,
noble musical and technical control. His opposite number,
the gifted Giacomo Lauri-Volpi, went in for rafter-shaking
top tones, held at epic length, rather than any searching
dramatic art. Less brash, more balanced was the singing of
Beniamino Gigli, geared to lyrical rather than clarion sound;
but he too skimmed the emotional content of much of the
music he sang, relying on sobs stacked by design, as though
grief might possibly be packaged. That his art should have
proved so incomplete, given his extraordinary voice and technical control, remains one of the still bitterly debated cases.
His opposite number, Tito Schipa, an artist of the Valletti
type but with rather more vocal metal to fall back on, was
able to surmount native drawbacks through taste and imagination. A depressing picture. Why could not the more naturally
endowed have come to terms with themselves?

And, finally, to anticipate the early days of Rudolf Bing,
there was Mario Del Monaco, an artist of golden promise.
We all knew even then that he sang too loudly, but this was
occasioned by mechanical trouble rather than conceit. He
simply had a hard time producing his tones *piano* and con-
fessed: "Non voglio castigare la voce" ("I don't want my voice
to take a beating"). This all-important defect aside, Del
Monaco appeared to have everything: musicality, temperament, good acting ability, a fine appearance onstage. For a
time it seemed as though the *piano* syndrome was being resolved; and in the title role of *Otello* he achieved some
beautifully equalized singing. But old habits, plus what must
have been a basic gallery complex, won out; and Del Monaco

passed from loud to shouting. Still later the blight of the 1940's caught up with him, as it did with most other imported artists (war rigors?) who had started at that time. Listen to most Del Monaco recordings today and you will hear a forcing of tone that makes the blood freeze; but remember, in case you did not hear him in those early performances, that here was a tenor of ambition, of goodwill, a performer who learned (if not always mastered) French and German in addition to his native Italian, a man who began with full integrity. One is sorry for later developments.

Ljuba Welitsch—who of those present at her New York debut as Salome will ever forget it? The evidence is all there in the superb recording of Strauss' finale that she made with Fritz Reiner and the Metropolitan Opera Orchestra. Hers was one of those rare voices—beautiful in itself—on which the owner, of top intelligence, could play as on an instrument, neglecting no possible nuance, no detail of light or shade. The ability to characterize became, in the case of Welitsch's Salome, an attribute almost of genius. She did not look at all convincing on stage, at least not for me. Instead of a teen-age princess—lithe, passionate, incipiently depraved—she suggested some old stroller from off the boulevards. But when Welitsch began to sing, Salome came alive for most of us as never before nor since. This was the authentic, palpitating sound: youthful, perverse, implacable. . . . And there was something else, luxuriously disturbing, absolutely animal that I have heard from no other artist. Where so many performers playing *femmes fatales* extend themselves ridiculously, go much too far in an effort to project the aura of sex, Welitsch had not to labor at all. Voluptuousness—real, not contrived— oozed from every semitone of that uniquely sinful voice. The acting, in spite of her grotesque appearance, was good, complemented the vocal magic. Still this was a performance that emphasized *tone,* played upon in the finest operatic sense. Welitsch's other roles at the Metropolitan—Aida, Tosca, Donna Anna, Musetta, Rosalinda—were to occasion strong arguments, and she too succumbed to that career blight of the '40's which had overtaken principally her Italian colleagues. The departure, in view of her accomplishments, seemed tragically premature.

One must in fairness to this era at the Metropolitan remark that standards of orchestral playing rose immeasurably as opposed to the sloppy sounds of Gatti's later years; that the caliber of conducting (Bruno Walter, Fritz Busch, Fritz Reiner, Sir Thomas Beecham) was vastly improved; but we are here concerned with singers and the stage. Again, in justice to a much criticized management, one should point out that the war years in general brought a decline of singing through most of the operatic world. Only in this country, and largely by the efforts of Edward Johnson, had a new crop been nurtured. Europe seemed bled; and it was not, coincidentally, until the advent of Rudolf Bing as general manager in 1950 that the international prospect improved. What started the surge? This can no more be answered than the question of what had begun the decline. One can only speculate, dimly, that with the passing of those war years, the lifting of anxieties from the towns where they had reigned, a fresh generation of European singers came better equipped for long careers.

Into this postwar situation was to be injected a prominent new blood strain, Spanish, reaching a climax in the 1960's.

There had, of course, been prominent performers from Spain in previous years, but never with such abundance. Teresa Berganza, Alfredo Kraus, Pilar Lorengar, Giacomo Aragall, Montserrat Caballé are now all artists of consequence; and it is my contention that despite the furor over Renata Tebaldi and Maria Callas in the 1950's, Victoria de los Angeles really carried that decade. But more of the Spanish ascendancy later, and back to early singers in the Bing regime.

One thinks at once of Cesare Siepi, brought in as a very young artist for the opening performance of that regime, *Don Carlo,* to replace Boris Christoff—kept from coming through passport trouble. Siepi, in this country by chance for a San Francisco debut, was signed by the Metropolitan on short notice. He triumphed and he grew. The voice, more lyrical than forceful, has not retained its pristine gloss; but the artistry of this basso has brought other, compensating pleasures. Refinement of style and diction, first-class musicianship, command of the stage continue to mark him as a valuable and important performer. He is the most aristocratic among Italian singers.

Regrets: the arresting theatrical talent and basically agreeable voice of Delia Rigal, the Argentinian soprano featured in that same opening performance, with gifts which, for reasons unknown, were not to develop along the lines one awaited; the brief but noteworthy career of the Italian baritone, Ettore Bastianini, cut short by untimely death; and the artistry of George London, interrupted in its prime by an illness that compelled him to give up singing. One has vivid memories of London as Boris, Amonasro, the Dutchman, Amfortas, Mandryka. The dark quality lingers, the presence comes freshly to mind.

Observations: those opposing divas, Renata Tebaldi and Maria Callas, more properly a pair of artists set up in needless conflict by their supporters. With the exception of a few roles in the Italian repertoire common to most sopranos—Tosca, Mimi, Butterfly, Violetta, Fedora—their choice of parts has been different, their vocal timbre not at all similar, their temperamental outlook poles apart. Finding each of them incomplete to a degree, I used to think of what an ideal combination their best qualities, rolled into a single performer, might make: Tebaldi's sound, Callas' imagination. And then I remembered G. B. Shaw's riposte to Mrs. Patrick Campbell when she proposed an heir that would unite her beauty and his brains: what of the ghastly alternative?

To lead off with Tebaldi, for she was the first through the sheen of her early recorded *Butterfly* to attract international attention, we have an artist with almost all the gifts that shape a great career. In 1955 when she made her Metropolitan Opera debut (she had appeared previously with the San Francisco company), Tebaldi confined herself to lyric roles, sang lyrically, thought lyrically. The sound of the voice was fresh, creamy, effortless. A statuesque woman of natural beauty, she radiated directness. Musically, she had a tendency to lag as if, from the beginning, she disliked navigating beyond certain speeds. And on the stage one missed a strong identification with the role. We were hearing Tebaldi, an attractive performer, rather than Mimi or Violetta.

At that time the voice had a brilliant edge, infrequently used, which served in moments of climax. As a decade went by and Tebaldi attempted parts calling for more dramatic weight and color, the edge began to take over in everything above *mezzo-forte*. The top grew harder, less secure. Despite these setbacks, Tebaldi was to remain a sovereign artist within her sphere. But a sense of adventure did not engage her. She sang opera in no language but Italian. Music even moderately contemporary never crossed her path. Nor, with the exception of Rossini, do the rare masterpieces of her own land seem to have drawn her. Only *Adriana Lecouvreur,* a turn-of-the-century bonbon, was to find her relatively far out.

After a vocal crisis during which Tebaldi withdrew briefly from the stage, she returned in improved condition, but not with the lyrical voice that had first brought fame. Full dramatic singing involved her now. Gioconda, probably the heaviest and most punishing role in Italian opera, became her property at the Metropolitan. She was also, in passing, to record that steely aria from *Turandot,* "In questa reggia." With the assumption of Gioconda, Tebaldi took on an impetus, one might even say vehemence, that became her in the theater. Her presence, formerly placid and gracious, developed a thrust nowhere evident before. Yet the new personality, while describing a wider arc, had not enough magic to compensate. The celebrated sheen was gone.

Why, then, Tebaldi's continuing popularity? The answer lies in two words: star quality. From the audience standpoint, this would imply memories of better days for both artist and listener (those first, youthful moments of rapture behind the rail, cheering a singer in her prime); an exemplary spirit of loyalty and zeal; a heart that leaps at the sometime resurrection of gorgeous tone; a mystic, undeviating absorption with *the name;* the temptation for younger fans to jump on the bandwagon; and a basic love, well earned, for the sovereign personality itself. Tebaldi has been cited as one of four established divas in our time, along with Birgit Nilsson, Leontyne

Price, Joan Sutherland. She shares with them the common ground of past achievement, present magnetism, unfailing command of style. But what of the communicative flame? In my own Pantheon I should enshrine performers less squarely oriented, better able to beam toward the listener an image of what opera poetically is about.

And it is on this basis, of course, that I stub my toe in trying to evaluate the art of Maria Callas. Surely there has been no singer of our time more perceptive, sensitive, musical, able to enthrall her admirers with the subtlest of nuances, tonal or dynamic. Yet in her quest for perfection, in the convulsing search to translate through an imperfect vocal medium the poetic drive that impels, Callas has all but torn herself apart, pursued by vulnerability and fury. Personal crises ought not concern us here; still the damage they inflict on tone and performance must be reckoned.

Callas has been compared, as a singing-actress, to Mary Garden, one of the great practitioners. But Garden, conscious of hostile vocal boundaries, never tried to cross them. She sang no roles that were, generally speaking, beyond her vocal skills. Moreover the Garden quality at its best was luminous and appealing, small-scale, perhaps, alongside the celebrated voices of her time, but clearly an attractive sound.

With Callas, on the other hand, a solipsist urge to encompass everything, delineate every kind of soprano role by stretching her resources unstintingly, has led to vocal woe. On the way, some mighty moments: a spectacular Violetta, a first-rate recorded Tosca (with Victor De Sabata conducting), and —I am told by those for whose judgment I have respect—a memorable Anna Bolena at La Scala. My own experience of Callas ranges from the early days in Mexico City, when she

was heavy and plain, to her first New York *Norma* and a
final *Tosca* by which time she had become—through a will of
iron—sleek and handsome. Even in her youth the top could
be abrasive. I recall a Mexico City *Puritani* (1952) and, later
that same season, a *Lucia* with the extreme high notes already
giving signs of strain.

Yet in the same performances one heard magical glissandi,
the chromatics matched like pearls. And much of the legato
singing was beautiful, surmounting a timbre that would
seem to be an acquired taste. The purity of Callas' intention
in those spun-out lines, her knowing treatment of the text
brought high pleasure. Of her famous perceptivity, I must
own to finding it didactic rather than spontaneous. Whereas
Kappel or, in our time, Ludwig would *convey* like a stab
wound an emotional reaction born of interlocking poetry
and music, Callas would comment on it, underline, and—in
unrivalled flashes—*illuminate*. The result bore witness to a
commanding intelligence; but, providing an aureole for the
performer rather than a force moving outward, it did not
often have the power to transport.

On one point concerning Callas there can be no debate: her
sense of musical adventure, her desire to roll back the limits
of today's shrunken repertoire. It was through her initiative
that several neglected masterworks of the *bel canto* era came
to life. We got to know, in her vital performances, large-scale
operas by Donizetti that had been only names in reference
books for more than a century: rare and important scores by
Cherubini, Rossini, Bellini. I found her less imposing in
standard works, always expecting a superb *Traviata*. But
whatever the issue, no project of this artist lacked distinction.
There was always some compensating factor to establish class.

And, as a sign of ultimate importance, I have never known a voice that could simultaneously enchant so many listeners and alienate so many others. Some magnetic fluid must have been contained in those tones, the power to attract or disaffect beyond that given any rival singer.

Callas has been hailed as a great actress. I should prefer to call her exciting, spectacular, with a drive more studied than visceral, rather too elaborately worked out. Disagreeing, it should be noted, are throngs of informed opera-goers who admire Callas in every respect. She remains, even while inactive, the most widely discussed soprano of the century.

The art of Victoria de los Angeles is, to begin with, fresh, limpid, elegant . . . but it goes beyond that into dimensions unexplored by most of her listeners. During her Metropolitan years she was constantly overshadowed by warring divas. She had no claque, no publicity. The criticism was voiced that she lacked temperament in the theater, belonged on the recital platform rather than the operatic stage. And yet, I believe that when all the returns are in she will have been accounted the most consistently satisfying artist of her time, the mid-century decade.

There was in de los Angeles a certain reticence mistaken by the uninitiated for slackness. She simply refused to overstate, to bend a tone or phrase out of joint, to exaggerate an emotion. Balance, in the most classical, Mozartean sense, was her keynote—a concord of lovely tone, suitable gesture, poetic sensibility. De los Angeles was no singing-actress in the tradition of a Lehmann. She approached, rather, and often transcended those wonderful memories of Rethberg; sang in that same poised tradition; acted better. It was the musical suggestion, the tone, the color that counted with this great Spanish artist. Her repertoire was formidable: the young Wagner heroines (Elisabeth and Eva), Gounod, Massenet, Debussy, Verdi, Puccini, Rossini, Mozart, all sung with the utmost verve and subtlety. On records, a stunning Bizet and Falla as well. Although the top was not ideally free, the range of the voice proved extraordinarily effective, from the high-lying brilliance of a Manon to the dark and delicious innuendos of a Rosina in the original mezzo key. Every word, in every language, was sculptured; the sung note was an extension of the word.

De los Angeles was a purely lyrical artist. She could probably not have portrayed a villainous or malignant character onstage. Charm, radiance, pathos were her sphere. And she always convinced. Lest her acting remain underrated, let me recall a moment in *Faust* when she ranked with the best. It was in the final scene, as produced by Peter Brook. Marguerite had already died. Her body lay hunched on the floor of the prison. And suddenly it seemed to rise from out of itself, walk resolutely toward another world. The sense of exaltation here conveyed was worthy of the finest actress. An impeccable feeling for mood had carried her through. Above all, this artist was never a "gut" performer. She won no frenzied, irresponsible cheers but, rather, the gratitude and admiration of all to whom the opera house is a temple, not an arena.

Through much of her career, de los Angeles has played opposite another patrician singer: the tenor Nicolai Gedda. His intensity has not always approached that of the great Victoria; he has let two or three of his rôles, notably Faust and Don Ottavio, slip into routine rather than creativity; yet he brings to many parts (among them the definitive

Roméo, Werther, Nemorino of our time) a glinting elegance of style, conquest of mood, resourcefulness of bearing that give him special rank. Like de los Angeles, Gedda is essentially a lyricist. His tone, when not forced, can be ravishing. He remains a performer for the listener who weighs and discerns.

As Franco Corelli does not. One *feels* with him or against him, in spite of him, because of him. He registers impulse rather than considered thought—which in some reaches of the repertoire comes off as an asset. This tenor has much that is legitimately going for him. His greatest disadvantage lies in the scruffy band of followers who claim him as their own, interrupt every performance in which he sings with shouts and yells, convert the opera house into the facsimile of a boxing arena. He does not need them and indeed has gone beyond them; for the fact is that, with all his appalling mannerisms, Corelli has travelled far and is still progressing. He may end as an artist of class.

Consider the voice: the finest dramatic instrument of our time, clarion, ringing, appealing to sophisticate and beginner alike. When, as increasingly happens, it is used to convey the music's inner meaning rather than Corelli's passing mood, the result can be overwhelming. The sound is generous, free, often noble. Less happy are the occasions on which leading tenor hang-ups, remembrances of *politeama* style—top tones held ridiculously long, volume dropped suddenly from *forte* to crooning *piano*—take over. And the Corelli acting style is apt now and then to seem narcissistic, with Franco apparently more in love with himself than with any romantic opposite number. Yet the outlook is not too bleak. Corelli has learned to take direction, as with a recent *Cavalleria Rusticana* in which the *régisseur* (Zeffirelli) successfully made him part of the action, turned his presence to the benefit of the drama. This singer has come so far and so fast that one must now suspend previously unfavorable opinions. Whether he will ever break through the traditional mold, give up the quest for applause, place his considerable gifts entirely at the service of music and drama is something which no one familiar with the opera house would dare predict.

In contrast to Corelli, his colleague Carlo Bergonzi seems the more scrupulous artist. The voice is first-class, with a lovely, ingratiating timbre. Bergonzi's phrasing, rhythm, enunciation are exemplary. On stage, unfortunately, he lacks charisma. Recordings are his best medium. Yet such taste and tone are not to be discounted in the theater.

With Jess Thomas, the American tenor, excellent in Wagnerian roles, temperament and imagination balance a limited instrument; while it is often the other way around with his contemporary James King, of splendid voice and placid outlook. The ideal combination would seem to have been effected in Jon Vickers who, at his best, sings up a storm. His Peter Grimes is unique in its power; Don José, Énée (as heard in a Covent Garden *Troyens*), Samson, Siegmund are strong portrayals. Every now and again Vickers goes a bit arty, worrying the phrase line, slenderizing his *pianissimo* to the vanishing point. Hopefully this is no more than a passing whim in a man who has achieved so much.

I can recall from the early years how many top sopranos used to sing the youthful Wagner heroines. Let a *Lohengrin* be announced, and as Elsa we would be offered Maria Jeritza, Elisabeth Rethberg, Lotte Lehmann, Maria Müller, Grete

Stückgold, to name several leading performers of the time. Today we have no Elsa. Leonie Rysanek, the nearest candidate, finds the part too lyrical for her growing dramatic powers. Elisabeth Grümmer, a lovely and finished artist, is unfortunately at an age that no longer corresponds. And so the crisis goes with Elisabeth and Eva as well. The singers who now attempt these intimate roles are either grand salami or small beer.

We fare better in German opera with that narrow stretch of road between the lyric and heroic known as *spinto*. I can think of no bygone Senta comparable to Rysanek's in theater magic. And the Sieglinde of Régine Crespin is on a par with the best from the recent past.

The weightier soprano parts in Wagner are, of course, well cared for. In Birgit Nilsson our generation has an Isolde and Brünnhilde of immense vocal powers, stunning musicianship, good acting ability, who fills the theater with epic sound. No matter what one's preference—the monumental or the tenderly drawn—one cannot take this superb artist for granted, do less than revere the phenomenal voice, the preparation and intelligence behind it. The rest is a matter of listener's taste. Nilsson's Isolde, wonderfully sung, lacks for my ears some of the shifting resonances implicit in the score. Moments dramatically introverted, darkly hued, appear not to draw her strength. More ideal, the spacious sonorities of a Brünnhilde. In related works by Strauss her Elektra triumphs through grandeur and thrust; her Salome is card-indexed by a prevalently Nordic gleam (as in her singing of much Italian opera). During the years since her Metropolitan debut, Nilsson's expressive range, mastery of nuance have broadened immeasurably . . . in conflict at times with that great but unyielding organ itself. Her most successful rôle would seem to be Turandot, in which—during the scene of the riddles—the majestic voice soars with coruscating volume above tenor, chorus, orchestra in a giant arc.

The big tone—in a warmer coloration—has also been associated with Eileen Farrell, who sings a good deal of Wagner in concert form, reserving her appearances in the theater for Gluck (*Alceste*), Verdi (*La Forza del Destino*), Ponchielli (*La Gioconda*). The voice is sumptuous, the musicianship first-rate, the style ample—but not, to my ears, very meaningful. No new light is shed, no searching interpretation drawn concurrently with the broad vocal brush strokes. Implicit, perhaps, is a lack of flair for the stage. And yet this singer has on occasion taken fire, created remarkable evenings. I find her Wagner synthetic but cannot soon forget a concert performance of Cherubini's *Medée* (in the Italian version) totally aflame.

Then what does one seek if not the grandeur of Nilsson, the amplitude of Farrell, in the singing of Wagner? Or should I say *whom?* By way of suggested answer, three artists from my personal Pantheon—Christa Ludwig, Leonie Rysanek, Régine Crespin—in whom the expressive element dominates. They color, communicate, ring myriad changes of mood. Every one of them has a technical hang-up of sorts, unimportant alongside their glow, identity, dramatic truth.

Crespin's sound is the most exotic: a voluptuous dramatic soprano, molten throughout. Chest tones are unfailingly rich; the middle like some dark, volcanic trysting place. Only at the top does the singer have occasional reverses—a suggestion of metal plate sticking up through the lava. But when Crespin is in form, the effect of this higher range can be grand. In-

WITH LOVE

Gertrude Kappel as Isolde

Ezio Pinza as Don Giovanni

Elisabeth Rethberg as Donna Elvira

Friedrich Schorr as Hans Sachs   Karin Branzell as Brangaene

Frida Leider as Leonore *(Fidelio)*   Lauritz Melchior as Tannhäuser

Lucrezia Bori as Manon

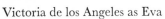

Victoria de los Angeles as Eva   Nicolai Gedda as Lenski

Galina Vishnevskaya as Katerina Ismailova

Christa Ludwig as The Dyer's Wife *(Die Frau ohne Schatten)*

Leonie Rysanek as The Egyptian Helen   Régine Crespin as Ariadne

Birgit Nilsson as Turandot   Rosa Ponselle as Rachel

WITH ADMIRATION

Kirsten Flagstad as Elisabeth

Lotte Lehmann as the Marschallin

WITH AFFECTION

Maria Olszewska as Octavian   Maria Jeritza as Sieglinde

Giovanni Martinelli as Eléazar

Giuseppe De Luca as The Barber of Seville.

Lawrence Tibbett as Simon Boccanegra

John Charles Thomas as Germont

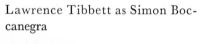

Alexander Kipnis as Gurnemanz

Ljuba Welitsch as Salome

René Maison as Herod

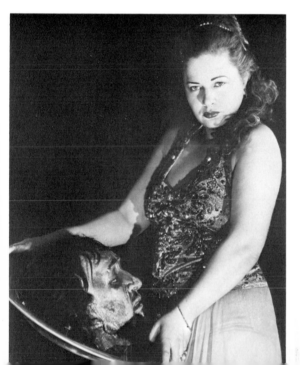

Bidu Sayao as Violetta

Jennie Tourel as Adalgisa

BOTH PHOTOS: OPERA NEWS

Jussi Bjoerling as Gustaf III
(*Un Ballo in Maschera*)

George London as Amonasro   Licia Albanese as Mimi

Cesare Siepi as Oroveso

Joan Sutherland as Donna Anna   Montserrat Caballé as Norma

Norman Treigle and Beverly Sills as Caesar and Cleopatra

Richard Tucker as Cavaradossi   Grace Bumbry as Lady Macbeth

Nicolai Ghiaurov as Philip II   Carlo Bergonzi as Manrico

Zinka Milanov as Aïda   Leonard Warren as Iago

WITH ESTEEM

Leontyne Price as Elvira *(Ernani)*

Renata Tebaldi as Maddalena di Coigny

Marilyn Horne as Isabella *(L'Italiana in Algeri)*

WITH REFLECTION

Franco Corelli as Don Carlo

Robert Merrill as Rodrigo

WITH EMPATHY

Maria Callas as Iphigénie *(en Tauride)*

stead of hitting the notes dead center, as in the Flagstad-Nilsson tradition, she *brings them up from under,* as one does the sediment from the bottom of a cup. Thus every color—dark, light, coffee, vermilion, chartreuse—rises simultaneously to the surface in one climactic blend, staggeringly beautiful in texture.

If all this sounds rhetorical, I shall remind those of you who were present on closing night at the old Metropolitan of a glorious moment: Crespin, in a scene from *Gioconda,* stirring her molten flow, making it rise, reach the top with a splendor that eclipsed the more predictable tones of every competing diva. The trouble is that this surging process seldom works. Much of the time it goes haywire, and then Crespin sounds metallic. But I am willing to settle for when it does come. Maximum highs can carry one skyward.

Sieglinde and Kundry—oddly, the two Wagner roles shunned by Nilsson—are Crespin's most convincing parts. Not that she is a great actress. Her gestures can be routine, her facial play lacking in mobility. But she is apt onstage, dominates the scene—and above all there is that voice with its bewitching viola quality. Her Marschallin, among the best since Lehmann's, ranks as a sensitive, carefully drawn portrait; her first New York Brünnhilde (*Die Walküre*) showed excellent promise, with pages yet to be filled. More controversial is her Tosca, which I enjoy, but my friends do not. Too uneven technically, they claim . . . and they are probably right. At this time of writing, Crespin is in vocal trouble—a condition one hopes might soon be remedied. Whatever the outcome, one cannot withhold gratitude for the many superlative evenings rendered.

The art of Christa Ludwig is more poised. There are no such discrepancies as with Crespin. And the sound, if less exotic, proves in the long run more rewarding, for it is allied to that intangible which, in the case of Gertrude Kappel, I have called the psyche. Indeed Ludwig is the present-day embodiment of almost all that Kappel stood for in the past: color not as an independent force but emanating from the word: darkness of mood that underlies the light, depth of personality almost untapped, *les fleurs du mal* in a subterranean garden, their scent rising to dominate the fragrance from above. For all this, and the rare sound of her voice, Ludwig has been my favorite singer ever since a Redoutensaal *Figaro* in 1958. The role was Cherubino—hardly a test of arcane powers; but something flashed that night which, for lack of a better name, I shall identify as the signal spark, making contact with one's wavelength, radiating the phrase that becomes a life-long part of one. The spark is not beamed often. Prize it when it comes.

Yet Ludwig has a problem, regrettable not for what it leads her to do but for what it keeps her from doing. To understand this fully, one has to dip into the system of "category" or *fach,* as the Germans call it, that governs operatic casting. Usually the assignment of parts is rigid and specific; but certain roles along the border between high mezzo and dramatic soprano may be sung by one or the other: Ortrud, Venus (in the Paris *Tannhäuser*), Kundry, Charlotte (in *Werther*), Marie (in *Wozzeck*). One has trouble at times in deciding where mezzo color ends and dramatic soprano (both are dark) begins. And in the question of range—a good mezzo should have an adequate high C—they often overlap. It is in this no-man's-land, this "in between" that Ludwig has been enjoying her greatest success. And yet she has not, whether by accident or design, seemed content to stay there. The voice, once pure mezzo, has moved upward in center of gravity and taken on a brighter, more distinctively soprano tint.

That is where the hang-up comes in. Instead of crossing the border with despatch, Ludwig lingers at the sentry box. After mastering two important Strauss soprano roles—the Marschallin in *Der Rosenkavalier* and Barak's Wife in *Die Frau ohne Schatten*—she has gone no further, fallen back on the old mezzo repertoire to which, in truth, she is no longer ideally adapted. Many listeners object to the sense of strain in Ludwig's upper voice when she sings *Die Frau*. I love it: top intensity onstage, a thrilling sense of unpredictability (will she make it?) out front. Old reliables, after a while, can turn one off. Ludwig never. Expectancy, unanchored, runs high. . . .

As it does with the third diva in my Pantheon, least conventional of all—Leonie Rysanek. She is a rhapsodist, performing along broad dramatic lines. One feels, when she is at her best, that she sings *because she must*. This artist gives off a driving compulsion, a frenzy for opera that seems almost hell-bent. She is reckless, prodigal, spends of herself. The voice, unhappily, does not always render what she needs: the dark lower tones of Sieglinde, for example, are not hers despite consummate poetic intent; the technical rigors of an *Aida* Nile Scene may dry up some of the top sonorities. But when Rysanek sings Strauss, that upper third of her gamut, from E to high C, has a brilliance unequalled by anyone in the profession today. Her climactic lines as Chrysothemis cut through the *Elektra* orchestra with strength and beauty, her anguished singing of the Kaiserin's monologue in *Die Frau ohne Schatten* rides the vastest sonorities from the pit. Yet it should not be thought that she thrives on *fortes*—or on Strauss—alone. The opening of her Ballade in Wagner's *Dutchman,* soft and remote, appears suspended in space; the ending of her "Ave Maria" in *Otello* has its own murmured dimension.

So strongly dramatic an artist is Rysanek that at times she overwhelms and upstages herself, for with her, as with almost no other performer, the improvisatory element is uppermost. She has small interest in the routine, the standard. It is the feeling of the moment that carries her. Every role, and evidently every performance, provides a new fantasy outlet. I find her easily the most live of singing-actresses. Visually she is never less than satisfying. And the voice, though now and then veiled at its deeper end, has a sound invariably brilliant —jubilant or demonic, as the situation may demand—when it rings out above the staff.

The Strauss element in Rysanek brings to mind other noted performers who have made their mark in these operas. Rose Pauly, in the Johnson era, set audiences cheering for her Elektra, well sung but overacted; Astrid Varnay and Inge Borkh, more balanced dramatically in the part; Margaret Matzenauer, of grandiose voice and appearance—a frightening, depraved Klytemnestra, the nightmare queen that Strauss must have envisaged; Kirsten Thorborg, not always satisfying in Wagner and Verdi, also rising to the top in this role; Sena Jurinac, a cherishable Octavian; Lisa della Casa as Arabella, her one New York success, and Alfred Jerger, a

stunning Mandryka (he created the part) in pre-World War II
Vienna.

Of Leontyne Price—a great singer, first-rate musician and,
when the occasion is right, commanding personality. Verdi
and Mozart are her proving grounds. She sings them with
taste, splendor, and in the case of *Aida* and *Trovatore* the
surrender of self that marks the major artist. Yet most of the
time, despite her ease and skill before the footlights, I find
myself reacting exclusively in terms of voice, which, except
in coloratura operas, spells the end for a dramatically oriented
listener. There can be no doubt of Price's temperament, the
exuberance of her approach, but they are absolute rather
than theatrical. One often feels she might be better adapted
to concert than opera; and indeed Price is best served through
recording, so close to concert in outlook. Here that slight
detachment in the house yields to full vibrancy and presence
before the microphone. She remains, under any circumstances, a ranking performer, a vocal force. My esteem goes
to her, but my love to another soprano in this same *lirico
spinto* category: Galina Vishnevskaya.

On the surface, this Russian artist would seem to have a
less opulent voice than Price, and perhaps she does. The color
possibilities are limited: while not burdened with the hard,
"white" Slavic timbre given to many sopranos—and tenors—
of Eastern Europe, she does lack organically the means for
widely ranging shifts. But the Vishnevskaya tone, funda-
mentally beautiful, cannot be divorced from the music sung,
the drama interpreted. It is an expressive medium, used with
depth and intensity. On stage Vishnevskaya ranks as a diva in
the noble, non-exploitative sense. She is handsome, dynamic,

commanding, attributes not limited to the theater. Her performance in the Soviet film version of Shostakovich's opera, *Katerina Ismailova,* has set new standards for singers appearing before the camera.

The world of coloratura: the non-believer on duty opens his ears. And when the music is Handel's, as sung by Joan Sutherland or Beverly Sills, preconceptions change. The decorative and expressive are not so polarized after all.

Brilliance—speed and altitude—counts for most in this world, softened by sweetness of tone in the long lines. It goes back as a tradition to the virtuoso male sopranos and altos of more than two centuries ago. They were vain, they were dedicated, their vocal ambitions knew no bounds, leading to black comedy disaster on at least one occasion. Angus Heriot in *The Castrati in Opera* * relates an incident that took place at the San Carlo in Naples during the 1760's: "The young castrato Luca Fabbris, straining after a top note of exceptionally dizzy altitude, collapsed and died on the stage, to the consternation of the composer, Guglielmi, who had induced him to sing it."

Within fifty years after that, it was the *prime donne* who were straining after top notes—and surviving. High sopranos, agile mezzos prevailed. (Rossini also wrote for florid tenors.) The ladies were often given patterns suggesting insanity, with opportunities to wander, accompanied by flute, along melismatic bypaths. They conquered, and some of these pages are superb, with power to move as well as excite. The mad scenes from *Lucia di Lammermoor,* from Thomas' *Hamlet* (of later vintage) have remained more than display

---

* Secker and Warburg, London, 1956.

pieces, their roots deep in dramatic psychology. But other vehicles of the time were less imaginative, lay closed in by formula.

The conventional output waned, and inventive new writing for coloratura, such as by Richard Strauss in *Ariadne auf Naxos*, did not attract the average soprano. The public lost interest, except in a few fabulous stars, and forty years ago much of this repertoire stood in darkness. The scope, the incentive were shrunken. Melba, Tetrazzini, Galli-Curci had by then retired (coloraturas of glamorous sound, cautious taste). Lily Pons was in the ascendant and reigned for many years. The voice was small, the tones *in alt* effective; and in addition to her vocal assets, she contributed personal chic and commendable musicianship. Her roles were limited; no modern operas, no old ones, only a cluster including *Rigoletto* and *Traviata* (in both of which the heroines are really lyric, not coloratura), *Lucia, La Sonnambula, Linda di Chamounix, Il Barbiere di Siviglia* (with its soprano rewrite of the original mezzo part), *Lakmé, The Golden Cockerel.* No Handel, no Rossini other than the mutilated *Barbiere,* no rare Bellini or Donizetti, no Strauss, nothing operatically beyond 1883. Pons, a charming artist, was not to be faulted so much as the myopic arbiters, of the time. This was the situation in most operatic houses from the late 1920's until well after World War II.

Then, of course, came Maria Callas with a revival of little known, often fascinating *bel canto* operas. Not a true coloratura (refusing, indeed, to be limited by any one category), she mastered their decorative side convincingly. But it remained for Joan Sutherland, with a big, opulent voice of a type unknown to us, raised on Pons in the theater and Galli-

Curci on records, to bring ornamented excitement, in the best sense, to the old coloratura vehicles. The operas of Handel, long on the shelf, were to stir new interest in part through the brilliance, security and amplitude of the Sutherland tone. Together with her husband, the conductor Richard Bonynge, she worked for musical authenticity, an approximation of correct historical style. The results (on her part) were exhilarating. One had forgotten, or perhaps never known, the sensation induced by glistening roulades at full strength, top notes solid as the proverbial rock.

Much time has passed since her emergence. Audiences no longer respond so fervently to the revival of *bel canto* operas (except in the vestigial case of another great singer, Montserrat Caballé). Sutherland has pointed her repertoire toward weightier, more dramatic roles: an exciting Donna Anna, a rather faceless Norma—in this judgment I go admittedly with a minority group. She has been accused, perhaps *because of* her eminence, of many secondary faults: sliding, scooping, veiled tone, poor enunciation, and I suppose that most of these strictures could, to a degree, hold up in court. But they are paltry alongside the singer's phenomenal voice and handling of it, her skilful musicianship, growing sense of characterization, search for fresh material.

And now it would appear, from news releases, that she has been topped. Beverly Sills, a highly accomplished coloratura, has come on the scene with honors. While admiring tremendously the achievements of Miss Sills—velocity, musicianship, style, acting—I do feel that each of these artists holds attributes not owned by the other; that they deserve to share public affection rather than contend for it. As for voice qua voice, I still prefer that of Sutherland. Sills' is smaller, lightweight and attractive without being strikingly beautiful. Her precision, on the other hand, is greater; she darts, hovers, wings. Like Sutherland (they both divide this gift), Sills can also spin out a lovely melodic line. To hear her "V'adoro pupille" in Handel's *Giulio Cesare* is to have experienced a top moment in modern opera-going. The embellishments are crisp, lovely and apposite; the overall quality melting. And Sills has firm command of the stage, is a wise as well as appealing actress.

Yet when all the reports are in, I feel that the finest singer of *bel canto* repertoire is not Sutherland, Sills nor Callas before them, but Montserrat Caballé. In the tradition set by Callas, she is not, despite great flexibility, a coloratura in the modern sense but a lyric-dramatic with high grasp of the decorative. She has taken on the Rossini, Bellini, Donizetti operas as flesh and blood assignments . . . and on hearing her, one is stirred. The voice can travel from an almost disembodied *pianissimo* to a ringing *forte*, embrace nuance and agility. In recital or in concert opera Caballé cannot be surpassed. Her performances in the theater please me less, for the acting stays grossly unformed.

Like many other gifted singers, Caballé is unpredictable; she varies strikingly from one evening to the next. That her repertoire and interpretative range are broad (at least in theory) may be attested by a spectrum ranging from Rossini's *Donna del Lago* to Strauss' *Salome*. In practice, her talents answer best to those rôles that evoke a pre-Verdi past. She remains a glorious period diva.

Separate item: Elisabeth Schwarzkopf, the most controversial of artists: the voice to be voted yea or nay according to one's taste; magnificent musicianship; high communicative power; professionalism just about the best in the business; acting (again according to one's taste) either wonderfully detailed or regrettably fussy. In the first and last items I stand with the nays.

Other sopranos of interest (a list selective rather than all-inclusive): the veteran Lucine Amara, who improves with every season; Pilar Lorengar, an accomplished lyric performer; Teresa Stratas, sensitive in lighter roles (Gretel, Yniold), swamped in the heavy Tchaikovsky repertoire; Mirella Freni, appealing in Puccini, less so in Gounod by reason of faulty French; Martina Arroyo, of the sumptuous voice, standing with Evelyn Lear, a gifted singing-actress, somewhat in an updated Tebaldi-Callas disparity; Teresa Zylis-Gara, *lirico spinto*, who has brought new life to a previously neglected Elvira in *Don Giovanni*, and Teresa Stich-Randall, good singer, consummate stylist.

Rita Gorr is the last of the mezzo-sopranos with what the Italians, both whimsically and admiringly, call "balls"—that is, a forceful, commanding, almost virile voice and presence. Too bad the voice has overshot its mark, lost luster through pushing and driving. Gorr has an impressive stage presence and, at best, volcanic temperament. She is in the big mold, a tradition currently on the way out. In roles that demand this quality, Shirley Verrett convinces partially; Regina Resnik arouses respect; Irene Dalis at least knows what should be done, but none of these owns the elemental sweep.

We do, fortunately, have finely etched lyric mezzos, talents on a more intimate scale. Ebe Stignani led this list a generation ago. Janet Baker comes to mind today as the most distinguished, with Anna Reynolds a glowing possibility. Rosalind Elias, underrated on the present scene, has a well-composed voice, lovely presence. But the big accent presently among mezzos is on motorization, a conquest of speed and altitude in the coloratura tradition.

The Rossini-type mezzo in our time goes back, of course, to Conchita Supervia, who has become a legend. Listening to her records will reveal a strikingly individual flutter on the attacks (I write this in admiration, not irony), a velocity which, if not always perfect, seems power-driven, the product not so much of calculation or of technique as of an innate *need* for expression. In this she reminds me of Rysanek. Next, over a distance of several years, came Jennie Tourel, an artist of superb good taste, resourceful equipment, whose Rosina and Adalgisa still shine as models. And then Giulietta Simionato—talented, amiable, a bit deceptive in her handling of coloratura. She had temperament and drive; excelled in roles of larger mold (Gluck, Verdi, Massenet); but her delivery of Rossini tended toward elegant evasion. In tribute to her mastery of the theater, one must say it worked.

Teresa Berganza is more generally accepted as a skilled coloratura mezzo. . . . But for those who prize virtuosity and daring on a base of absolute solidity, there can be no rival—as of this writing—to Marilyn Horne. Her musicianship is phenomenal, her conquest of many styles overwhelming. And yet I must confess to being turned off by the commonplace quality of the voice itself. These are subjective thoughts . . . Simionato, for all her mechanical shortcuts, brought poetry. Horne is high-powered, muscular—in prose.

For really top coloratura mezzo singing in our time, one must turn to a surprising source: Christa Ludwig's Adalgisa in the second recorded version by Callas of *Norma*. The Ludwig voice, in recent years, has become more conspicuously soprano. As to the dazzling agility, I do not know whether she might match it today. But for sheer splendor—in context— this Adalgisa ticks off perfection.

One other mezzo-soprano must detain us, potentially a great one: Grace Bumbry. Why great? Because, essentially, she owns that rare gift of communication, that psyche-to- psyche transmission of which I have written at length. But with Bumbry the gift is more gleaming, flamboyant than in those I have named previously. She is able to magnetize a large public without arcane tuning-in.

Despite excursions into the deep contralto repertoire (Azucena) on the one hand and dramatic soprano on the other (Lady Macbeth), Bumbry is a true high mezzo, excelling in the same borderline territory (her best role—Eboli) as did Ludwig in earlier days. The timbre is dark, the expressive element firm and strong.

Here, too, a first-rate actress. That she almost brought off a Carmen (and was kept from doing so only by the impossible Barrault revival in which she was cast) is much to her credit. The Santuzza, too, must be reckoned an "almost" rather than a complete achievement, again for reasons beyond Bumbry's control. Santuzza is simply not a mezzo role. They all sing it—but insufficiently. When the climactic moments arrive, when repeated A's, sustained B-flats and a C are required, no mezzo—by the very nature of the voice—can be comfortable. It is one thing to encompass a top note, another to pour it on. Santuzza belongs to dramatic soprano—the electrically charged preserve of a Tosca, Gioconda, Turandot. One longs to hear Bumbry in a starring role which the voice finds congenial. Carmen was an excellent start.

Regrettably absent: Helga Dernesch, Gwyneth Jones, Magda Olivero, Anja Silja, none of whom I have heard in the theater. Other omissions arise from lack of empathy.

Tenor jottings: grateful memories of Ramon Vinay in his superb delineation of Otello. The tasteful singing of Sándor Kónya in the lyrical Wagner roles; his extravagant gulping in Puccini. Placido Domingo's winning vocalism in all but the heavy assignments that require him to force. The knowingly fashioned art of George Shirley, sometimes short on vocal sheen, compensating always with true theatrical elegance. Alfredo Kraus of the slender tone, ingratiating presence. Those new arrivals—Helge Brilioth, Wagner-Strauss tenor of fine promise; Luciano Pavarotti, a capable *spinto;* and Giacomo Aragall—handsome, well comported, musically rather remote.

A crisis of baritones. They all sing big, or practically all. Only a few are unconcerned with decibels: Hermann Prey, in his well etched Mozart characterizations, keeps down to scale with lyrical tone; Gabriel Bacquier, when not too carried away by Scarpia's villainies in *Tosca,* works pretty much for taste and balance; and Geraint Evans, an artist of enormous refinement, comes off well in every respect. Most others are trying for Judgment Day sonority. Sherrill Milnes, in prime condition, sings out prodigally. That his tones should cascade in Niagara-like plenitude is a matter of rejoicing to those who love the monumental in song. For others (myself included) who feel that gradation of nuance, finesse of shading—given a first-class instrument—are what opera singing is about, that wonderful outpouring loses some of its appeal in time. Peter Glossop, also lavish of constant climax but more the artist, and Cornell MacNeil, accomplished singer with a voice now divested of its early rugged drive, share the same outlook. The results are often grand but, except in the case of Glossop, only slightly varied; and I am glad, on listening, to have heard Giuseppe De Luca, Richard Bonelli, Herbert Janssen (when not saddled with heroic assignments unsuited to him), John Charles Thomas, lyric baritones who as a rule did not drive their voices, brought home to the opera-goer their linear, unforced approach with every phrase.

Ironically, the one baritone division in need of big, clarion tone—Wotan, the Dutchman, Hans Sachs—finds itself today on the anemic side. Anyone with vivid memories of Friedrich Schorr in these roles, of Rudolf Bockelmann, Joel Berglund, Hans Hotter, Paul Schoeffler, must of necessity look backward. George London, in the time allotted him as the Dutchman, gave promise for the other heroic parts as well; Thomas Stewart offers today an intelligent, well sung Wotan; Theo Adam,* a god dramatically compelling; but nowhere in sight is the Wagner baritone who can exult and despair, freeze and melt—the heir to mighty predecessors.

The personal reservations department: Tito Gobbi, once a

---

* Several months after writing the above, I attended a Munich *Meistersinger* with Theo Adam that gave extraordinary proof of his growth as performer. Adam's voice may still be on the light side for Wotan; but his lyrical, sensitive, yet richly sung Sachs compares, in its very individual way, with the best in one's experience. Here is an artist heading toward the top.

major singing-actor, now blending rusty sound with aggressive theatrics; Dietrich Fischer-Dieskau, justly renowned in the German lyric repertoire, awkward and contrived in the Italian dramatic—judging by his recorded Scarpia, Macbeth. For these impieties, may I be shriven.

And an admiring glance at those artists who have renounced the lyrical not for the monumental but the manly and direct, whose voices, not always beautiful in texture, convey at all times the essence and intensity of the music they sing: Sesto Bruscantini, Tom Krause, Eberhard Wächter, Walter Berry.* That exhausts the eligibles. Not one *baryton Martin* in sight to shoulder the high-lying, almost tenor-like French roles with anything like the trim, sensitive timbre required: Hamlet, Hérode, Valentin. We are served unremittingly with beefsteak when more subtly composed dishes might satisfy.

And the state of bassos: only a few years back, most performers in this category were pushing for the high bass-baritone parts, driving their sonorous centers upward (understandably, in view of the acting opportunities offered by such famous *cantante* parts as Boris Godounoff, Mefistofele, King Philip II, Don Quichotte). Many bassos still aim for the top . . . but a fresh supply of "black," deep (*profondo*) voices have been tapped, new artists discovered who have helped the medium toward a broadly based rebirth.

And in this regard, one of the thrills in a lifetime of opera-going came not long ago at a Metropolitan *Don Carlo*. The scene: the King's study. The participants: Nicolai Ghiaurov as Philip II, Martti Talvela as the Grand Inquisitor—two outstanding bassos of whom Ghiaurov was the known quan-

* And the late Hermann Uhde.

tity. He sang from strength to strength, the voice opening out with every fresh emotion—a truly marvelous performance. And yet the possibilities of this part, its great *cantante* traditions had been familiar to us, charted by other famous bassos. Not so with the Grand Inquisitor. Written for an organ deeper in range, darker in color than the King's, the part is usually taken by a sung-out baritone adept at talking the music's lower reaches. When Talvela sang the role on this occasion, from pedal E to high F thunderclap, a whole facet of opera came alive, the authentic world of *profondo* sound. And the contending bassos not only illumined Verdi's sonic genius, they brought new vitality to an entire *fach*.

Again, in *Das Rheingold* one has heard a recent pair of giants, Fafner and Fasolt (Karl Ridderbusch and Talvela), produce sounds of a depth and luxury seldom attempted in the opera house. This could be, in the best sense, the age of the basso. When Siepi is in form; when the magnificent Boris Christoff concentrates without mannerism on the task at hand; when even he is surpassed by Ghiaurov, complemented in turn by Talvela; when such capable artists as Ridderbusch, Giorgio Tozzi and young Ruggiero Raimondi share honors with the upcoming John Macurdy, a new era seems at hand.

Ghiaurov, Christoff . . . names with which to be reckoned. Yet I should put beside them—and in some respects beyond them—an American basso on whom recognition is only now bestowed: Norman Treigle. I have on occasion doubted a theatrical detail or two (the result of stage direction imposed against the grain); but when he is master—and that is easy to detect—the grand design of any score he undertakes comes through as unique in our time. The acting is flawless; the vocalism, that of a fine *cantante,* reaches the same level—powerful, musical, unforced. He is a basso for today.

There remains the world of the character singer: the bright, sometimes vocally edgy *soubrette* (Despina, Musetta); tenors who depict the treacherous, comic, bizarre (Mime, Shuisky, Guillot, Vašek, the Astrologer); baritones alternately villainous and clowning (Alberich, Beckmesser); and bassos mostly buffo, sometimes sinister (Dulcamara, Pasquale, Bartolo, Varlaam, Prince Khovansky).

Among the tenors who undertake these parts, there has been none as yet to replace the late, fabulously versatile Alessio De Paolis. Gerhard Stolze, leader in the Wagner field, is given to caricature: a whining, disquieting artist. Among the baritones, Gustav Neidlinger offers a strongly sung Alberich; Benno Kusche, a first-rate Beckmesser who never overplays. Succeeding Baccaloni, and perhaps excelling him vocally, has been Fernando Corena, a versatile technician and a singer of heart.

Sometimes celebrated artists essay these character roles. Ljuba Welitsch once undertook Musetta at the Metropolitan, and the results are still a conversation piece. That fine singing-actor of a generation ago in Vienna, Alfred Jerger, played Beckmesser with enormous success. On other nights he would appear as Wotan or Mandryka. Geraint Evans is a notable Beckmesser of today and an equally fine Don Pasquale. And if I may be permitted to close the circle by going back to an artist singled out toward the beginning of this chapter, Ezio Pinza—a towering Boris Godounoff—was incomparable as the vendor of elixirs, Dr. Dulcamara. Within the elaborate protocol of operatic casting, flexibility remains at the service of the great.

4

THE CONDUCTORS

I F SYMBOLS be needed, the opera conductor's baton has served for generations as a token of his power. Yet the baton, in the sense of scepter, did not always reign in the theater. Not until about 1815, when Ludwig Spohr and Karl Maria von Weber—both crusading composer-conductors —instituted modern methods of orchestral direction, did centralized command enter the opera house. Throughout the eighteenth century, authority over the performance had been divided between the concertmaster, guiding the orchestra with his bow, and the composer seated at the cembalo, cueing and reinforcing the singers. The concertmaster led from a first-violin part. Knowledge of the full score was confined to the composer at his keyboard.

After establishment of the new set-up, more theoretical than real, came the long tunnel. For every great composer-conductor in the theater such as Spontini, Meyerbeer, Berlioz, Wagner, there were hundreds of plodding time-beaters eager to placate the reigning prima donna or star tenor. The pay was sufficient; the job carried a certain prestige; and in some of the less complex orchestral scores a permissive beat could work no harm. Celebrated singers made most of the decisions, generally with expertise and discretion.

Yet the inevitable revolt, the final establishment of the conductor's authority, was to arise on several fronts. In Germany philosophical insistence brought it about. A new concept of *the total art work* (music, drama, acting, physical production, all on the same plane of importance) invaded the repertoire: Wagner, as theorist, in the ascendant. For the most effective production of his music dramas, control became centralized, passed into the hands of a single man—the maestro.

Elsewhere on the Continent power headed from stage to pit for practical rather than aesthetic reasons: the growing number of players. In Paris the works of Meyerbeer, given with pomp and splendor at the Opéra from 1831 till the end of the century, required, among a host of ambitious effects, an enormous orchestra. By the 1860's, when Wagner descended on the city to produce his new version of *Tannhäuser,* the French house owned the mightiest instrumental group in Europe. Conductorial acumen—backed by an able if unprincipled management—had made it so.

In Italy the serious operas of Rossini, long before Meyerbeer or Wagner, had begun to lay stress, through their big choral ensembles, on the musical director's skill. And with the rise of Verdi a performing aesthetic developed which, though not a copy of the Wagnerian total art work, paralleled its outlook in many ways. The great Italian in lifetime kept a jealous eye on his operas and the theaters that performed them, demanded optimum results not only from leading singers but from scenographers, from the radically evolving orchestra and the guiding figure at its head. Following his death, Italy sank back temporarily into a vocal preserve.

No such pendulum swing took place in central Europe once the principles of Wagner had been established. The one-time rebel was to become Tradition incarnate. Even Mahler and Richard Strauss, noted path-breakers in their own music, held faithfully to the line as Wagnerian conductors. The road had been opened for them, the rules laid down before the start of their careers. The performing need in their time—and they met it spectacularly—lay not for innovators but consummate technicians, sovereigns of a theater already made over to them by Richard the First.

On the Italian scene, Arturo Toscanini enjoyed no such advantage. After having reached the top as an exponent of Verdi, he found himself working in a void, his master's concept of theatrical unity hovering near disuse. Famous names, star personalities were again in command. Integrity, daring, egotism led this maestro to overthrow them as a caste, substitute with sublime but often constricting results the dominance of one artist—himself—in every corner of the opera house.

And so there came into being the dictator-conductor, with great virtues yet many of the faults previously deplored in star singers: authoritarian outlook; limited receptivity; will to dominate at the expense of others. In our own time his power has been largely eroded, owing to the rise of the stage director, the new colossus on the scene; but a few dictators of the baton linger on, at least vestigially. Their fate was pinpointed over a decade ago at a Metropolitan Opera piano rehearsal when a famous diva clashed with her maestro. "That's all the shit I'm going to take from you," declared the great lady. "I'll have you fired." The maestro, it should be noted, was not dispossessed. He is still around. But his divine right cracked that day like Wotan's spear beneath the brusque and ugly impact of Siegfried's blade.

Under the order now passing, the conductor was the artistic conscience of the performance. He determined the style, pacing, overall standards of taste. And if he was reasonably capable of meeting his singers and players half-way, able to elicit rather than bludgeon, nothing was lost in spontaneity. It should be remembered, if one is to grasp Toscanini's outlook, that general education and musical inventiveness did not rank high among orchestral performers in the Italy that saw him emerging. They were, on the whole, people who invited discipline rather than persuasion. Even when the Maestro first came to the United States in 1908, professional attitudes—though more evolved—were far from what they have become in our time. Three generations of American musicians, trained impeccably since then in our conservatories and universities, were to broaden their life style; the Maestro, understandably, less so. Although he mellowed with age to a marked degree, Toscanini remained essentially himself—commander-in-chief—until his final days (1954) with the NBC Symphony, hurling strictures in a manner that players would have accepted from none other. His years, his position, his greatness carried the day—and the performances were memorable. It is, however, an undisputed fact that his frequent rages, his uncontrolled quest for perfection inhibited certain of the singers who appeared with him toward the last, put them in the position of doing less than their potential best. Fear can paralyze, at least in part, the vocal cords.

The first contact between singer and conductor in the preparation of an opera should take place ideally at private coaching sessions, with none present except the maestro himself and the artist who is at work with him. Most opera conductors are able pianists. They have had to be, coming up the hard way as rehearsal assistants; and they can handle the keyboard dynamically. (There is in fact a maestro's style of playing: forcefully accented downbeats, clearly etched harmonic changes, unbroken structural line; above all, a maximum of musical support, minimum of notes.) Such early encounters are to be sought; but most conductors, beset by crowded schedules, cannot find the time. And so one discovers in almost every opera program the phrase *musical preparation by* . . . , which means that a capable assistant has coached all singers individually until they are ready to take part under the maestro's baton, with the assistant at the piano, in their first group rehearsal.

Here, at a relatively intimate meeting without orchestra, adjustments can be effected between conductor and singers, disagreements ironed out, sources of friction eliminated. Afterward, when players fill the pit, it may be too late for one side or the other to concede. Nerves are on edge, reputations at stake, that cursed intangible known as prestige rules the roost, and there may be war. This type of conflict happens not too often in German or Russian opera, since these repertoires are generally symphonic, voice and orchestra tending to interlock (exception must be made for earthquakes in the days of Chaliapin, an epic force onstage, but the tremors have long since passed). In French opera as well, singers and maestri are bound to concur for the sake of dramatic unity. It is the Italian repertoire that still provides a battleground between pit and stage. Even now, conductor and star may race from rehearsal to the general manager's office to argue in his presence over how long a top note ought or ought not to be held. The winner is usually the one with the larger take at the box-office.

There was a time when the soprano, among these battling creatures, would play winged victory. More recently it has been the tenor. We have lived to see even the mighty Stokowski interrupt the progress of *Turandot,* arrest the passage of his hands (and of the score) in mid-air following the last top note of "Nessun dorma" so that the vocalist might reap applause. Lesser conductors too, in current Metropolitan productions of *Tosca, La Fanciulla del West* insert pauses where they do not in fact exist so that the claque, the cliques and the clucks might have their day. Perhaps when this has gone too far, another Toscanini will appear. Troubled times bring their own correctives.

At least we are free of that odious custom known in Italy as the *bis,* practiced in all but the most august theaters. By audience fiat, any number chosen for an encore must not only be sung a second time but *acted all over again.* . . . "Vendetta!" cries Rigoletto, hurling Gilda some moments later to the ground. The curtain falls. Uproar out front. Shouts of *"Bis! Bis!"* The curtain is raised and the two singers, like automatons wired for sound, go through the same routine note for note, gesture for gesture. The conductor is powerless, in provincial companies, to intervene. He must bend the knee or perish. And in New York, at our

leading opera house, we are witness to another, blander tradition at work: the maestro's timid wait in mid-performance
until the last splatter of applause—spontaneous or paid—has
died away before going on with the show. This is obsequious-
ness become ritual. Time to break it up.

From the technical standpoint, it is infinitely easier to con-
duct in a major theater than in a modest one. The stakes, of
course, are higher, the responsibilities tremendous . . . yet
possibilities for disaster in the larger house are minimal.
Everything in a provincial auditorium except the singing and
scene-shifting (there is little stage direction to speak of) de-
pends upon the maestro. One imprecise flick of his baton
(conductors, being human, may flub in their attacks just as do
singers) and the ensemble—that unpredictable union of
voices, instruments, and colliding psyches—no doubt poorly
paid and under-rehearsed can go up in smoke. With equal
danger, a principal may in a moment of panic plunge three,
four, sixteen measures ahead. Without the presence of a fully
qualified and resourceful prompter, almost as commanding
as the conductor himself, calling shots from that tubular box
flush with the stage and pressing down into the orchestra
pit, such a situation can spell chaos. Any opera conductor
worth his salt should, in principle, be able to head off the
errant singer, jump with the orchestra to safety (in a first-
class house the players themselves are so well routined they
can zoom to the rescue automatically), but too much gets
sacrificed in toll of nerves. This responsibility is generally
assigned to the prompter,* who will guide the singer from his

* In most large theaters. There is one notable exception: the New York
City Opera, where prompting is opposed in principle.

lair below the stage, speak the key words in advance, indicate
the musical entrances, keep the soloist on the track.

A well organized house will also have several *sostitutti*
(assistant conductors) in the wings, not only to direct offstage
choral and instrumental runs, but also to provide the technicians with lighting and curtain cues on the beat, send
singers "on" at moments designated in the score. Until about
a decade ago, offstage conducting shaped up as a hazardous,
nerve-wracking, unrewarding job. If all went well, the assistant's ability was taken for granted. If some mishap oc-
curred (and this used to be all too likely, with the assistant
having to peer through a hole bored in the scenery or dangle
from a ladder above the curtain line to catch the conductor's
beat out front and transmit it to a brass band in the wings),
there would be hell to pay in the chief conductor's chambers
after the performance. Today the *sostitutto's* lot is, in the
long run, no less bleak but at least his working conditions
are more serene. Closed-circuit television relays the conductor's beat from the pit to monitors placed throughout the
wings. No more peering, no potential for fumbling. All this,
naturally, in the wealthier, better organized houses.

What then, in view of toil-reducing technological assis-
tance, remains the function of the maestro in charge of a
first-class opera performance? I base my answer, admittedly
written in sand, on the current Karajan pattern. The man is
there to animate, guide, control. The singers are his wards,
the orchestra and chorus his subjects. In time not far back
the stage director also bowed to conductorial wishes. But
since the recent emancipation of the *régisseur* and his rise to
power, Karajan and a few other conductors have undertaken

to ride both horses—drama and music—rather than give up a scintilla of their authority.

The opera conductor's preparation? Most of the great ones have come up through subordinate posts in the theater, have acquired alertness and flexibility at basic level, the knack of adjusting to all situations.* The outstanding talents will leave, to develop along symphonic lines; but inevitably they return, at least for part of the season, as guests, master directors, sovereigns of pit and stage. Among them, past and present: Mahler and Walter, Reiner and Szell, Busch and Klemperer, Europeans who learned their craft in state or municipally supported theaters. Conditions have been less favorable here. We possess few opera houses, none subsidized, all—for the past forty years—financially in hot water. Owing to the uncertainties around us, assistants tend to remain assistants, or if they do progress to a comfortable post, they cling to it as to a spar. No outside ventures, no symphonic training or conducting in the big style. They remain routiniers the rest of their lives, ready for any technical emergency but shy of venturing toward a broad, free interpretation. Color and dash are not for them.

On the other hand, conductors raised in a strictly symphonic milieu often have trouble adjusting to the theater. Sometimes even the most famous can fall short. I recall, in this light, a production of *Turandot* at the Metropolitan directed by Leopold Stokowski. Audience susceptibilities were kindled on opening night by the maestro's hobbling dramatically across the pit on crutches (following a serious leg injury), emotions ran high. And indeed from the standpoint

* Arturo Toscanini, in whom flexibility was the sole missing virtue, developed his operatic skills not backstage as assistant, but in the orchestra pit as 'cellist.

of orchestral sound, listeners that evening were not dis-appointed. It was on stage that nagging lacks made inroads: ragged choral attacks, poor synchronization and pacing of solo singers. One realized the maestro was confronting Puccini's score with alien equipment, armor of the concert hall. And this lapse may be explained. All of Stokowski's previous operatic conducting—including the great perfor-mances of *Wozzeck* in Philadelphia and New York—had come under special auspices, giving non-repertory works with countless rehearsals, calling soloists and chorus from outside to make music with a group permanently under his com-mand: the Philadelphia Orchestra. Performance conditions had been perfect, rarely the case with an opera company that functions as an active daily concern. Rehearsals are few on that other shore, instant adjustment to singers essential; and above all there is need for lightning speed—in terms of the theater—for transmitting the conductor's every impulse stage-ward.

One more wrinkle in this same communications problem relates to Zubin Mehta—symphonic maestro with good knowl-edge of the vocal score—whom I have heard bear down over-poweringly on solo artists in *Turandot* and *Aida* until their dignity and initiative were in retreat. And I have been present at a *Tosca* that crumbled in the face of a similar grand push. Conductorial *chutzpah* in the opera house without the theatrical adroitness to back it up cannot succeed. In the concert hall, where the issue is less sensitive, Mehta works handsomely.

Another maestro given to symphonic attitudes (though with less flamboyance) is Lorin Maazel: an impression, one hastens to admit, based only on appearances of some years back at the Metropolitan Opera. Maazel has in all probability become more flexible since then as music director of the Deutsche Oper in Berlin. Imperious was the word for that New York *Don Giovanni* and *Rosenkavalier* of long ago— haughty and remote. Yet his recordings of those elusive one-acters by Ravel, *L'Heure Espagnole* and *L'Enfant et les Sortilèges,* shine out, are scintillating and masterly. One awaits him in further operatic engagements, a performer not to be underrated.

Last among this group that has impressed more strongly on the concert platform than in the orchestra pit: Claudio Abbado. Unlike his contemporaries, he has sought accommodation with his soloists and, in the process, gone flaccid (at least on the evidence of a Metropolitan *Don Carlo*), a matter once again having to do with theatrical values, their indispensability to the musical impulse.

Thomas Schippers, rare among today's younger conductors, combines operatic routine with symphonic élan; and he is still maturing. His Rossini, Donizetti, early Verdi glow with the colors of an era in which he seems to find aesthetic center. Best of the Schippers projects so far is a recording of *Macbeth* marked by dynamic commitment. As yet his readings of French and German repertoire—*Manon, Der Fliegende Holländer, Elektra*—are less convincing, though one feels even here a knack for dealing with the basics of theater.

Most of these assets, plus a broader repertoire, keener sense of pacing but minus Schippers' ebullience and personal warmth may be found in the conducting of Julius Rudel, guiding force of the New York City Opera. Rudel, an organizational genius, has been responsible almost single-handedly for the development and artistic success of the company that he heads. Just as its program is varied, trim and effective, so—in a complementary sense—remains his conducting. Any performance he directs is a reservoir of security, poise and destination. He has probably mastered more styles and periods than any musician now before the public. I find the sound rather gray and impersonal, the scope none the less impressive. A genuine theatrical craftsman, Rudel has confined his efforts to opera in spite of a marked symphonic flair, has never really left it.

Another fine musician who does commute between the two media with ease is Erich Leinsdorf. He began in the opera house as coach, rehearsal pianist, assistant conductor, then became maestro; developed on the concert platform; now plays either field with mastery. His gifts are more widely ranging than Rudel's, tinged with greater imagination, illumined by deeper structural insight. And yet both men are alike in their indifference to (or perhaps disapproval of) the Dionysiac element that plays so vital a part in theater music. Leinsdorf's performances are superbly well organized, frequently moving, but rarely sensuous. Dabbling in sonorities is not his game.

Nor is it that of the school from which he sprang: the central European *kappelmeister* tradition, sober and solid, producing as its golden image a George Szell (in whom leavening elements of fantasy intermingled with sterner, less mutable qualities) or, along more conventional lines, such able but hardly enkindling talents as William Steinberg, Josef Krips, Max Rudolf. These are the men who always deliver, never fail, yet (except in the shining case of Szell) render rather than recreate. They stem from a culture now defunct in which order, down to the last detail, was king, regional rather than cosmopolitan values the standards.

Consider the impact of Leonard Bernstein, representing all that these conductors are not. Visually informal to the point of controversy he brings a personal conviction, musical strength that transcend this surface detail, a communicative warmth that sweeps an audience along with him into the interior of a masterwork. Though raised in the concert hall, Bernstein is so innately theatrical that the transition to opera came with overpowering speed and rightness. A born master of whatever medium he enters, in no matter how brief or concentrated a time, Bernstein stands outside the usual pattern for conductors of opera-to-symphony-back-to-opera. He came into the opera house full grown with a glorious *Falstaff,* marked by polish as well as energy; a generally praised *Rosenkavalier;* and a *Cavalleria Rusticana* (dead end for any conductor—full of technical traps, few compensating outlets) rather loud and slow. One may cite a few preliminary performances by Bernstein some years ago at La Scala, but the truth is that, operatically, he has just arrived. The theater is his natural home; his musical qualities make for first-class performance; and he works consistently well with singers.

Inversely to every conductor of imagination in the opera house, either regularly or as guest, we have dozens of routiniers capable only of propelling the performance, not of giving it life-breath. These are the men who have found a snug berth in the theater, stayed on, never let go. Under the present system at the Metropolitan where quality conductors apparently for budgetary reasons are passed over in favor of top-salary singers, many lesser maestri who would normally wait attendance in the wings now wield the baton out front. It was not always so. Musical assistants in time past were limited to the rehearsal room or, at best, to directing popular-priced Sunday night concerts (long since discontinued) at which ten or twelve secondary artists topped by one or two stars would declaim their favorite arias to an oddly mixed public: earnest young listeners, misty-eyed old timers, and a swarm of raffish drifters who roamed the seventy-five cent standing room.

Ranged above the assistants and associates on today's musical roster are two or three staff conductors of full rank, one of whom, Fausto Cleva, can excel more glamorous guests on occasion. Though lacking a bit in freedom of style, he has excellent communication with the stage, good orchestral command and, above all, a miscroscopic knowledge of the vocal score. Buoyed by such assets, he succeeds at times in those very operas in which a Stokowski or Mehta might fail. It has been said that Cleva is not popular with singers, that his approach tends to be overly detailed and exacting. This may account for some rigidity in performance; but he is a mainstay in the running of a big theater. His colleague, Francesco Molinari-Pradelli, also owns considerable technique, less interpretative flair.

Among the top-name conductors, Karl Böhm continues to be active on both operatic and symphonic fronts, with results that I confess are something of an enigma to me. When in the mood, as at almost every performance of *Die Frau ohne Schatten,* he conveys high theatrical intensity along with a special feeling for balance, texture and central form—attributes also to be found in his superbly recorded *Tristan und Isolde* with a Bayreuth Festival cast. Yet there have been sterile readings of *Don Giovanni,* coarse-grained accounts of *Der Fliegende Holländer.* Who can accurately probe the recreative mind, explain the difference in performance it engenders? I should say Böhm is stronger on response than on initiative, swept along—when at his best—by such scores as *Tristan, Die Frau* that contain irresistible currents in themselves. This, of course, is speculation. Whatever the truth, symptoms remain of a talent divided, never quite of a piece in range and direction.

I regret, as a New York-based listener, the absence of Rudolf Kempe who after a wonderfully evocative *Ring* at the Metropolitan some years ago withdrew because of ill health. Here was a conductor of elegance, perception. And on the contemporary scene I should welcome a guest appearance by Wolfgang Sawallisch in significant works of the German repertoire. He has recorded creditably. A single "live" *Tannhäuser* should tell all.

Which leads us, via Wagner, to the greatest operatic conductor of our time, Herbert von Karajan. His knowledge, command, flexibility, sophistication are linked in one star-flaming trajectory. Along with a virtuoso grasp of orchestral sound, Karajan penetrates the drama in its every aspect (a musical achievement not to be confounded with his lesser gifts as stage director). He is, in the best professional sense, a modern mind.

His intents are suspect, like those of all famous performers who have drawn an audience cult. One wonders how much calculation is intermingled with his art. Yet Karajan, though possibly contrived, is never flamboyant. Not in the pit. His much publicized life outside (private planes, Moroccan bank accounts) is responsible for a certain "image" rather than any eccentricities of performance. His approach is sober, his gestures spare. True, the Karajan scale of sonorities for a recent *Walküre* ended up as an audience conversation piece. Chamber music textures in voice and orchestra are not readily associated with the turbulent first act of Wagner's music drama, and they occasioned a shock. Karajan pulled back in later performances, revised the balance. His judgment is not here defended . . . *but at least he had a point of view.*

This fixity of purpose marks the great opera conductor, carries him above all phases of technique once they have been secured. With Bruno Walter, in a former generation, *melos* came first. Mood and song stood in the ascendant. Everything else was subordinate. For Sir Thomas Beecham the ruling element was color; not the gloss applied to a product already prepared, but organic texture—music and drama in their most sensuous application. (Among a sector of today's conductors headed by Pierre Boulez it is struc-ture—architectural mass rather than mood or color—that shapes interpretation.) With Toscanini and Reiner it was rhythm, not so much the obvious central beats as the inner, pulsing life of a phrase. Both these great men had other obsessions as well: Reiner's fire-and-ice, almost crystalline treatment of the vast Straussian orchestra, Toscanini's impas-sioned unfolding of a simple melodic line; but rhythm came first, the inevitable pacing, overall sense of destination. It is not easy, with the prevailing memory of this rhythm, to recall the color of the Toscanini orchestra. What stays in-scribed on the inner ear of those who heard him is the momentum, the whiplash drive, the taut line leading to the climax.

And with Toscanini one passed automatically from rhythm to tempo—the one area of performance in which every maestro is bound to differ. Many opera composers, it is true, have left precise markings of the speed at which their works should travel; but these are seldom observed to the letter. In so human an art as opera the metronome cannot rule alone. Important side issues enter: the size of the stage, sustaining power of the singers, pulse rate of the conductor himself. In short, physical conditions do much to shape the going tempo. This question remains sensitive to the highest degree. A shade too fast or too slow may spell disaster for an otherwise splendid performance. If err we must, better to sin today on the rapid than the dragging side. No audience likes to come unglued with the music. Toscanini as he aged (was he attempting to disprove the years?) leaned increasingly toward brisker tempi.

On occasion the contrast in pacing between one conductor and another can almost pass belief. Under the baton of Artur Bodanzky, the first act of *Tristan und Isolde* used to last roughly an hour. In the celebrated recording by Wilhelm Furtwängler, with Flagstad as Isolde, the same act runs almost half again as long. Imagine this difference in the theater, where every minute imposes its own identity! Clearly Bodanzky's reading, though cogent, was too fast. On the other hand I find Furtwängler's inadmissibly broad. The minutes lag, they buckle under, they die. What assails us is that central European malady, elephantiasis of tempo, too often confused with grandeur and amplitude. The same disease afflicts much of Otto Klemperer's current work for the stage and used to ravage the *Elektra* and *Rosenkavalier* of Hans Knappertsbusch. One should note, however, that Knappertsbusch's lingering tempi, fatal to Strauss, served well *in his hands* for Wagner. This veteran knew how to fill the spaces in *Parsifal,* impregnate them with poetry.

Another concern of the opera conductor, too often ignored, is balance. Of what avail the noblest singers if they are blanketed by monster sonorities from the pit? This issue has been met head-on by theater designers ever since the days of Richard Wagner who not only covered the orchestra at Bayreuth but sloped his players in terraced formation, strings nearest the surface, heavy brass and percussion beneath the stage. The effect, as those familiar with Festspielhaus acoustics will attest, is magical. Yet few modern pits are masked (except, oddly enough, for today's musical comedies). Opera conductors prefer the limelight; the public enjoys profiles and batons, makes a habit of gazing among the music stands whenever boredom takes over onstage. And so a compromise device has been effected: the adjustable floor, working either in separate sections or as an automated unit. In an opera house with this type of mechanism, Mozart and Debussy will find their niche just below audience level, Wagner and Strauss near the bottom of a shaft, Verdi in the space between.

There are times, however, when mechanical balance can fail. The dispersion of sound is not foolproof, and the conductor must remain alert. Even when Wagner is played in the sub-depths, certain climaxes, if not controlled at the source, can shut out the hardiest voice. And in Strauss, at no matter what distance beneath the stage, brasses and winds still pose tremendous problems that must be solved in advance, worked out at rehearsal by maestri who know and care. One wonders if it was by more than chance that three conductors, Fritz Reiner, Fritz Busch, Karl Böhm, notably sensitive to the interaction of voice and orchestra should all have been attached in prewar days to the old Dresden Opera, now a ruin. The performing traditions of that house, dating back to Karl Maria von Weber, must have been fabulous.

If even the improved modern pit offers problems, the reader can imagine the difficulties of conducting opera in the many convention halls and high-school auditoriums of this country that have no facilities at all. Players are seated on the same level as the audience, an improvised rail separating them from the first row. Brass and percussion, untamed by architectural devices, lunge at the listener. Woodwinds erode the singing voice, strip the enamel from every note that leaves the stage. To effect a proper balance under such conditions is nearly impossible. If the instrumentalists surrender abjectly, their attack, bounce, intensity are gone. If they defy the stage and play at full blast, the singers are dead. The most scrupulous adjustment of tone is needed, as in fine quartet playing. A skilled conductor can achieve this balance in principle; but the ratio of rehearsal hours (time out to weigh every chord) to the one or two performances involved makes of his work an economic folly.

I have already mentioned, as part of a conductor's preparation, the need for flexibility. A more fundamental term might be empathy—total identification with singers, orchestras, settings, lights, of which alertness is only a part. Moreover this identification ought not be limited to intellect. Full communication is called for, visceral as well. I am not here plumping for vulgarity or flamboyance—only for aesthetic honesty, the transmission through mind and heart of what lies in the music. While Latin maestri may respond too exuberantly in this respect, bending a score out of shape, north Europeans and Americans are apt to worry it with excessive caution. For a sound middle path, I commend the art of Colin Davis.

One brief reservation: Davis seems out of touch with edges, hard and soft. His *Wozzeck* lacks the bite, the acid imparted to it as a matter of routine by a veteran like Böhm. His conducting of Berg is compassionate, straightforward. In his Berlioz, on the other hand, I sometimes miss the sheen, the lambent elegance of a Beecham. He does not play *with* the music, strike from it that improvisatory spark.

And yet . . . how many conductors of our time have the strength, the rugged uplift of this man in action? Nineteenth-century attributes, perhaps, but of enormous help in the theater. By virtue of his personal exaltation, Davis succeeds in raising *Peter Grimes* from an admirable stage piece into one of the unforgettable experiences. Who, having heard this maestro in the pit and Jon Vickers at his best onstage in Britten's opera, does not feel he has been guided across a particular frontier, landed where the music on its own might not otherwise have propelled him? And, in the process, a score undefiled, ungunned, ungoosed. In the case of Davis, when all channels are open, the life force lifts one high.

I am not similarly moved by Georg Solti, a conductor with splendid technical command. In concert repertoire, with the Chicago Symphony, he has drawn highest praise. Why, then, the reserve (at least mine) about Solti in opera? The negative reaction stems largely from his recordings of the *Ring, Salome, Elektra,* with their abdication of the right to mold sonorities of his own, balance instruments and voices perceptively, work for organic tone. Studio forces have taken

over instead with crude, blow-up insistence. Nor have I
been overwhelmed in the flesh by an adroit but undistin-
guished *Tannhäuser, Don Carlo.* Solti has gathered fame,
racked up achievement in the opera house (at Covent Garden,
on a long-term basis, rather than in his passing appearances
at the Metropolitan). Of this there can be no discussion. It
is simply that for one subjective listener his finer qualities
have not yet chimed.

The effective conducting of Italian opera no longer demands a Latin birthright. More than three decades ago
Walter, Reiner, Busch came through with their top-level
Verdi for an international approach; and the trend continues. Karajan conducts Mascagni and Leoncavallo at La
Scala, which is like carrying coals to Newcastle; Bernstein has
scored with *Falstaff* in New York and Vienna; Schippers, one
of the better interpreters of Rossini and Donizetti, directs
this repertoire here and abroad.

Italy, however, has continued to produce maestri of merit
and in some cases of grandeur. The late Victor De Sabata,
supremely sensitive musician, conducted historic performances of opera at La Scala, both in person and on discs.
Vittorio Gui, scholarly and stylish maestro of the same generation, has presided over Verdi and Rossini not only in his own
country but at the Glyndebourne Festival as well. Those
opera-goers with lives wrapped around the Metropolitan
have grateful memories of Tullio Serfin, less the mercurial
maestro than the complete, authoritative coach, the tasteful
senior conductor through whose efforts the Italian (and on
occasion German) repertoire came to glowing realization.

There are several younger talents now at work. Noblest

among them is Carlo Maria Giulini, a conductor of taste,
principle and—when the spirit moves him—passion. The
Giulini recordings all bear these qualities, as did, I am told,
a stupendous *Don Carlo* at Covent Garden. On leading his
only New York opera—*Le Nozze di Figaro*—in 1968 during a
visit with the company from Rome, he brought intimacy
and charm (frustrated in part by the troupe's inferior
orchestra) to the performance along with a *spirituel* quality
that suggested an updated Walter. Further in the same series
Bruno Bartoletti, directing Verdi's *I Due Foscari,* showed
valor and imagination, proved himself a conductor of class.
He is, for part of every year, attached to the Chicago Lyric
Opera. Among the many other Latin imports appearing with
a certain regularity in this country, the most notable is Carlo
Felice Cillario, born in Argentina but sprung from the
Bolognese musical action, a capable, dedicated maestro; and
of the American opera conductors cast in Italian mold,
Nicola Rescigno has created his own artistic world in Dallas.

I am at a loss to understand the scene in France. Jean
Fournet, with first-rate recordings of *Pelléas* and *Louise* to
his credit, keeps to the background. He officiates every year,
it is true, at the Teatro Colón in Buenos Aires; but Paris
seems to withhold approval.* Pierre Boulez, once of the Opéra,
has moved on to other, international terrain. And it would
appear that Pierre Dervaux, a long serviceable maestro, has
dropped out. Of young Alain Lombard, formerly of the
opera at Lyons and now at the Metropolitan, more time is
needed to form a just estimate. His work, uneven so far,
contains much exuberance but not always enough finesse.

* He has recently been appointed chief conductor of the Rotterdam Philharmonic.

Whom have we left? This would appear to be the era of Georges Prêtre, brilliantly gifted yet puzzlingly limited. Where orchestral effect is paramount—as in *Samson et Dalila, Dialogues des Carmelites*—his ability to draw dazzling tone, whip up exciting rhythms has served him well. But in recorded versions of *Les Troyens* (excerpts) and *La Damnation de Faust,** as well as in Metropolitan Opera performances of *La Traviata, Tristan und Isolde,* he has skimmed the surface, substituting speed and brio for the poetry lying at the core of these works. A *Parsifal,* also in New York, fared somewhat better but could not in itself dispel the impression of a maestro disturbingly erratic.

The coda is left to the personalities themselves. Despite the presence in our time of many distinguished maestri, it is the custom—and conspicuously at the Metropolitan—to splurge on divas of both sexes, scrimp on musical directors. Some day, when this point of view has been revised, when it is discovered that conductors are not accessories but animating forces, the repertoire, the audience, the performance may be revitalized.

* French tempi for Berlioz, under the spell of the late Charles Munch, have leaped to dizzy, hot-rod excess. More healthy, the balancing trend of Colin Davis and Alexander Gibson across the Channel toward an electric but reasonably contained Berlioz in the tradition of Pierre Monteux. In this same area I have not yet heard the work, generally admired, of Charles Mackerras.

5

THE PRODUCERS AND DESIGNERS

Politics bubble. Opera, in the person of historic façades, seems frozen. Yet it is affected no less than are affairs of state by changes in fashion—only at a slower tempo. The entrenched, the apparently irreplaceable fade in time. And just as the divine right of divas was abolished at the turn of the century by a power play from the pit, so are the prerogatives of today's conductor being whittled by the new top man in the house: the producer.

The prestige he wears like a suit of armor was not always so highly burnished. Nor is his title in itself of long standing. He was once known as stage director. The man, within available memory, was a staff employee backstage—usually a retired singer with knowledge of theatrical practice gained at first hand. Waving his arms from the wings to guide roving "supers" thrust on stage with barest preparation, he made no attempt to solve or even pose psychological questions, probe the motivation of plot and characters, spin a dramatic mood growing out of the music. The stage director of those days was no theorist. It was his duty to supervise traffic, keep it from getting snarled, see that established routines went on without interruption.

And those routines! Among others, kept up for years: El Remendado, one of Carmen's smuggler friends, sententiously declaring "Le fait est délicat," then giving his colleague, El Dancaïre, a playful kick in the rump; Beckmesser, distraught from a beating suffered the previous night, going into a chain of contortions timed to coincide with every blithering *sforzando* in the orchestra; Gilda, just raped by the Duke, tearfully joining her father in a dressing gown evidently lifted from the Duchess. These belonged on the pile of dramaturgical garbage that used to be known as tradition.

It has been largely cleaned out, at least in the big houses. Only the bad aural smells remain. That wretched E-flat *in alt*, interpolated by so many dizzy Violettas as the curtain falls on Act One of *La Traviata;* another high-flying intrusion (this time a top B out of nowhere) for Des Grieux at Le Havre in Puccini's *Manon Lescaut;* these are testimony to rancid musical taste. Yet accept or reject this aesthetic, it is rooted in a longing—no matter how perverse—for vocal glamor, spectacular sound.

Most visual traditions in opera have no such leavening aim. They represent a shoddy, evasive shorthand whereby productions can be thrown onstage with little or no rehearsal, singers and machinists following patterns from across the years. A working knowledge of such shorthand, its able use in performance, does presuppose a brand of professionalism. The old-fashioned stage director knew his stuff; the performance always moved, was never—even at worst—obscure. But the drama conveyed no more than surface flow.

This type of direction, long gone from our major theaters, hangs on in many cities presenting opera briefly during the year. Rarely, even in the Italian provinces, does one meet with performances less enlightened, more anachronistic than in the plazas of America, always excepting those by a few companies with means and independent policy.

The new direction came first from Russia, not the stage of the Bolshoi, given then as now to grandiose productions, but from more emancipated groups. Stanislavski and his approach to the art of the actor—urging the performer to look inward, put the springs of experience at the service of rational interpretation—had left their mark not only on spoken drama but, incipiently, on a portion of the operatic world as well. Chaliapin, who understood this philosophy, practiced it individually long before it took popular hold. But his work, impressive in itself, sparked clashes. An isolated artist moving along novel paths could be accused—and was—of intransigence, of setting up a deliberate disharmony with his colleagues. The need was for a producer, a perceptive, dominating figure, to establish one style, one concept, with the cast fused into a single instrument of communication.

An opera lover's first encounter with a group of this type can be shattering. Mine came in adolescence, during a New York visit many years ago by the Moscow Art Musical Studio. They were performing a version of Bizet's *Carmen* which they chose to call *Carmencita and the Soldier*. Totality of approach prevailed, never contrived, blindingly new and different. The troupe employed a unit setting: arches in perspective that suggested according to the degree of light an aqueduct at the edge of a Spanish town, nocturnal recesses of a gypsy tavern, endless prospect of caves in a mountainside, formal arcades outside a bull ring. At every moment the visual mood came alive.* But more daring, for the time, was the rationale, the master plan linking spectacle and music. No hint of routine, of exhausted tradition. The drama ruled, with full illusion of spontaneity—actually the product of an all-encompassing will. Poetry and logic were as one. And that most idiotic of characters, Micaëla, did not set foot onstage. Her music floated from somewhere behind the arches as an expression of Don José's divided thoughts. The effect, in a musically satisfying and well sung performance, was overwhelming.

This basic look, but with dramatic techniques grown mannered, vocal results less rewarding, was taken up by several of the avant-garde houses in pre-Hitler Germany, later to find its way to the United States. Refugees brought it here. The excesses of the German system are well known and still with us (at least vestigially, in some of the older workshops dating from the '30's): a fanatical emphasis on movement, often at the expense of song; the manufacture of situations on stage to match every doodle, every bend from the pit.

Just as one does not judge a metal by its slag, a trend by its fringe, one keeps faith with the ideals that produced a *Carmencita*. The unity envisioned by Gluck and Wagner for their own works but never put into practice for *all* of the repertoire until after World War I is here to stay . . . until the next change of fashion. Today's producers are skilled and aware, limited only by a variable command of music. Many of them know the art well. Others, uninitiated in the reading

* Unlike a production of *Carmen* along similar lines devised decades later by Jean-Louis Barrault.

of score, think in terms of spoken drama, "legitimate" timing. Many chances have been missed. And yet so much has been gained. We no longer tolerate clutching and lurching on our major stages; we demand a motivated development of character, whether or not the librettist has obliged.

Organic commitment replaces the old-line stage direction, antiquated traffic control. The new approach deals with the basics of dramatic thought. And on those wonderful occasions when the producer reveals the structure as if freshly conceived, helps us toward a fresh emotional understanding, he takes his place beside the conductor as a fellow titan. The giants are now battling for first place in the opera house, with the producer apparently winning out. I am not sure, despite his frequent lack of musical knowledge, that this is bad. It may represent an indemnity for years of theatrical neglect, of emphasis centered almost exclusively on the score.

The title of stage director survives, but in a new and humbler connotation. Once the producer's work has been set, his duties at the house are ended. He will be off to other theaters, new fields of conquest. And an assistant on the regular staff will have taken notes for keeping the production in trim. This, in our time, is the stage director: a company man who re-rehearses the creations of others. No matter how diligent his efforts, details begin to be missed, the flavor dispersed. Unlike the conductor, who stands guard over all performances of a revival or novelty, the producer decamps.

But his prestige remains. It is not generally known that, according to protocol, his work stands protected against all revisions, even by the general manager. Understandings may be reached, suggestions adopted; but a big-name producer is secure against unwished for changes. If this seems high-handed and unreasonable, one might remember that, by the same standards, an impresario will never try dictating tempi to a conductor. By chance I have known only one who did. The next year, whether by coincidence or not, he was out of business.

Opera could not have gone on much longer in the theatrical vacuum that prevailed at most leading houses only a generation back. As in the case of Chaliapin years before, great performances by individual artists outstripped overall concept. Only two or three top producers—or stage directors, as they were then called—brought the spectacle into an affective relationship, dramatic and psychological, with the music: Lothar Wallerstein, veteran of the Vienna State Opera, his productions confined largely to Austria; Carl Ebert, pioneer in modern methods, working in Germany, England, Turkey; and Herbert Graf, young in the field when he already commanded stages in New York, Salzburg, much of Italy.

Graf, very active still as of this writing, was at the start labelled a rebel. Much of his early work courted the bizarre. He learned to temporize. Whether the renunciation came through changing values or dispiriting fatigue has never been made clear. One can only trace the parabola of his career, note the conservatism that was to become so prominent a part of it that today (linked perhaps to his role of impresario at the opera house in Geneva) his outlook would seem governed more by performing problems and their solution than by deeply felt convictions. Yet he has broken valuable ground along the way.

It took a new generation to bring off the complete metamorphosis from stage director to producer, the assumption of major prerogatives in the opera house. The breakthrough came, significantly, at a very special place: postwar Bayreuth, where the torn continuity of a world-famous festival had to be rejoined. Depleted resources, inability to raise the huge budget of former times may have prompted Wieland Wagner in the beginning to turn away from conventional elements of production. But his aesthetic went deeper. In shunning externals as practiced in the past, concentrating—with virtually an open stage—on what to him was the dramatic truth of the work, Wieland effected a revolution.

His use of symbolism may on occasion have seemed heavy-handed, the voltage controversially low; but these were minor phases in a project that wiped clean the tarnish from a masterpiece, brought it fresh performing glow. The molded scenery, though startling, was not entirely new. Adolph Appia, back in the nineteenth century, had worked toward total fusion of design with action and music. Neither was the virtuoso lighting, strikingly basic to Wieland's scheme. Distinguished producers in the theater, from Max Reinhardt to Orson Welles, had long before accomplished wonders in that department. The miracle worked by Wieland lay in the grafting of these elements onto the living tissue of performance, his ability to lead the artists themselves toward a new emotional grasp, musical projection that made him arbiter in all things.

Wieland's daring, the rightness of his approach are subjects better treated by those familiar with his productions over a long period. Mine is the task of placing them in perspective *outside* Bayreuth. His treatment of standard operas for the big German houses—notably Verdi in Berlin—

seems to have provoked resistance. The same methods used in his grandfather's works have drawn only praise.

And yet, since his premature death in 1966, how much of the new Wagner-Wagner tradition has survived? A *Lohengrin*, taken over during his final illness for production at the Metropolitan by an assistant, Peter Lehmann, proved not only disastrously static but raised the thought that time might be passing Wieland by, the hourglass of fashion running out more quickly than is its custom. My purpose is not to dwell on the lacks in a production that did not carry the master's full signature so much as to question the idea of transplanting *any* of his work—complete or denatured—from the atmosphere in which it was born.

The Wagner music dramas are only a part, though an important one, of opera. That Wieland excelled in their staging is not to be argued. His *Ring, Parsifal, Holländer* set new standards. The query remains: alongside the excitement stirred by this single medium, has he influenced production in general?

On the surface, our answer would seem to be, not much, for Wagner production is a specialized affair, and Wieland's only heir along these lines is Herbert von Karajan. And yet—a great deal. The nature of Wieland's dictatorship at Bayreuth, his personal command of all the arts entering into large-scale performance has paved the way for the scope and pretensions of many modern operatic producers, especially in Germany. A figure that comes to mind at once as embodiment of this authoritarian approach is Walter Felsenstein, director of the Komische Oper in East Berlin and, according to those who know his work well, a genius. He is, make no mistake, the boss. At his theater the conductor plays second in command; the singers rehearse tirelessly, often in full voice (the bane of every vocalist, who must husband the resources in his throat as does an investor his capital); and no work may reach the boards—down with schedules!—until the producer declares it ready. Call this despotism; but the results are outstanding.

To the producer's threat as a rising force, Herbert von Karajan, born to command, has responded by broadening his activities from pit to stage—with Wieland's *Ring* as his springboard. No grand innovator, he has worked along Bayreuth lines, adding well placed dynamics of his own. Designs are spare and symbolic, lighting largely on the obscure side. Two parts of the Karajan *Ring* have been seen thus far in New York: *Die Walküre* (offered first, out of the cycle's regular order) and *Das Rheingold*. The effect has been contradictory, like so much surrounding this great conductor: *Walküre* theatrically below par; *Rheingold* high on illusion. And the impression persists that Karajan is still learning his trade as *régisseur*. Would it not have been more valorous to seek and find his artistic counterpart, his theatrical double, a producer as fully in command of the stage as he of the orchestra?

The search for such a master producer would probably have led in the direction of Italy, once so laggard in operatic stagecraft and now in the forefront of musical theater. A few Germans of course stand out: Günther Rennert has a considerable reputation in Hamburg, and the late Rudolf Hartmann, on the basis of a warm-hearted *Meistersinger* experienced recently in Munich, must have deserved the praise that came his way. Sweden has given us Ingmar Bergman, film director extraordinary, in a stage production—reputedly first-rate—of *The Rake's Progress,* and Goeran Gentele*, a contemporary force in Stockholm noted especially for his mounting of Blomdahl's space opera *Aniara.* Yet the Italian approach, diversified, sensitive and vital, holds the mark in our time. It stems not from opera but the spoken drama, avoiding inflated tradition and embracing instead the clarity and elegance of modern Italian thought. Its leading exponents—Giorgio De Lullo, Luchino Visconti, with Franco Zeffirelli, a debatable third—are men of enormous musical awareness, trained in the theater. Visconti, of a patrician Milanese family long associated with La Scala, comes by this musicality as something in the blood. And in the case of Giorgio De Lullo, of a younger generation than Visconti, song is a reigning element.

I remember him well as an actor. It was in 1945, as a soldier in Rome, that I attended a performance of de Musset's *Le Chandelier,* featuring an actress then ranked as the Katherine Cornell of Italy, Andreina Pagnani. The play, translated from the French, turned on the relationship of an older woman with a younger man: Candida-Marchbanks, really, but with more poignant overtones. Pagnani was applauded; the youth of twenty-two or twenty-three making his debut was cheered. Giorgio De Lullo won every heart through not only his presence and his skill, but also the beauty of his singing voice. Certain melodies relevant to the plot were taken with a tenor *dolcezza* that lingers.

The musicality has continued. Now one of Italy's great actors, De Lullo has also become a formidable producer of both spoken drama and opera. An example of his work

---

* Gentele has recently been chosen by the Metropolitan to succeed Rudolf Bing as General Manager in 1972.

presented in New York by a visiting troupe from Rome during the Lincoln Center festival of 1968—the rarely given
I Due Foscari—radiated top intensity. To this little known
opera by Verdi, its architectural splendor dimmed by a confused and confusing libretto, De Lullo brought the clarifying
touch, the taste and verve of a master. His production of
Macbeth, offered by the same company at its home base, won
an even greater success. At this time of writing, he has been
engaged by the Chicago Lyric Opera for a new production of
Traviata.

During the same period at the end of World War II when
young actors like De Lullo and Vittorio Gassman were trying their wings in the Roman theater, Luchino Visconti was
already a distinguished director of plays. His drift toward
opera, given his musical indoctrination, would seem to have
been inevitable. At best Visconti captured its grandeur, less
the traditional dross. His accent, within a massive frame-
work,* lay on nobility of line, the pride of kings. With
knowledge and intent he held to the old style: singers well
forward for the great numbers, ensembles played for maximum depth.

The changing of tides in operatic fashion has today put
him in a rather baroque frame of reference. The larger-than-
life, massively noble has receded as an audience mandate.
During the same New York visit by the Rome Opera that
brought De Lullo's production of *I Due Foscari,* we had Visconti's version of *Le Nozze di Figaro,* preceded, with much
solemnity, by a statement that this was to be no Viennese
pastry-shop Mozart, but a thing of flesh and blood, vigorous

---

* Working in another, exceptionally lyric vein, Visconti helped make of
Maria Callas the unique singing-actress she became in full career.

realism. What emerged, with perhaps the most stunning scenery (designed by Visconti himself) ever on view at the Metropolitan Opera House, old or new, was a dramatic *infarinatura* of halcyon days before the French Revolution. Figaro himself was made into a surly Gérard, symbol of the servant with rebellion in his breast. In justifying this approach, Visconti invoked Beaumarchais, prophet of class conflict and author of the play on which the opera was based. What the producer had evidently overlooked in his source material was an account from Figaro's own lips ** of his hopeful beginnings in Madrid as a playwright, of hard times, falling into debt, giving up a literary career and migrating in disgust to Seville, where he embraced the profession of barber. In short, he was an intellectual. What we faced in this Roman *Figaro* was a know-nothing, a lout short on brains and long on temper. Visconti, despite protestations of realism, had presented him as a symbol—the exploited valet to the count; and it is on symbolism that Italian talent founders. The great conductors and producers of that nation have been at their best in the pursuit of clarity.

Least convincing to me of current Italian producers, but by far the most popular in transatlantic circles, is Franco Zeffirelli, once assistant to Visconti and now ranking commander on the scene. He is equally adept at direction and designing. Broad splashes of color bring excitement to his work, lend it a febrile quality synonymous to the uniniated with the molten flow of Vesuvius, the flamboyant Italy of the *bis,* or perhaps that Renaissance terrain—more in imagination than actuality—of romantic swordplay, spectacular love

** Not in *Le Mariage,* but *Le Barbier* of the same cycle.

and intrigue. Although Zeffirelli is of the theater, his mind seems largely cinematic, preoccupied with effect on a surface level.

That he can go deeper, on congenial assignments, and sometimes strike real metal has been proved by the success of a *Falstaff* produced for the Metropolitan Opera, a *Romeo and Juliet* for the Old Vic. At best he summons the poetry of motion, harnesses it to the richness of scenic backgrounds (who can forget the stage done in ochre for the Fat Knight's rueful monologue, "Mondo ladro!"?), creates a synthesis on the verge of the genuine thing. His singers, artfully grouped and cleverly moved, strike fire with the audience. Like the "well made play" of Pinero or Lonsdale which was good theater as far as it went, his more durable productions contain admirably tailored elements of drama, well cut pictorial sweep. What they do not offer, at least for me, is an excursion into the core.

Many opera-goers were startled by the failure of Zeffirelli's plush mounting for Samuel Barber's *Antony and Cleopatra,* with which the Metropolitan opened its new house, appalled at how the elaborate staging, overripe scenery obscured a score which, if no masterpiece, at least deserved to be heard. Although *Antony* was low ebb for Zeffirelli, his production of *Cavalleria Rusticana,* given at the Metropolitan in 1969-70, also raised questions of taste. It may be argued that any place of worship can assume majestic proportions, especially on Easter Sunday. But when a rustic * church looms cathedral-like over the landscape, when a modest religious procession takes on the magnitude of a coronation scene, when the gritty soil, ever-present poverty of a depressed area (for these details

* For this interpretation, note title of the opera.

in context see any movie on a Sicilian theme directed by Pietro Germi) are passed over in favor of staircase pageantry à la Godounoff, we know this is not *verismo* but swollen glands. In those phrases of the midway, Zeffirelli can knock 'em dead. He has what it takes . . . but what, in the production of opera as an art, *does* it take?

Giorgio Strehler, celebrated Milanese director for the spoken drama, is still finding out. A 1967 *Entführung aus dem Serail* given at Salzburg with Zubin Mehta in musical command, won him high approval. Gian-Carlo Menotti, who has long known, remains one of the most dynamically gifted *régisseurs* today. Italian producers may be controversial but never dull; and at their aristocratic best, as with De Lullo, Visconti, quite magnificent.

I cannot vouch for the musical backgrounds of Strehler or Zeffirelli because I do not have all the facts. Italy's other leading producers are, for certain, either practicing musicians or thoroughly sensitive listeners. That they have come out of the spoken drama and into the opera house is to their— and the impresario's—great advantage; but without a knowledge of scoring and structure they could not have gone on.

Too often in the world beyond the Italian theater producers of unproved musical background have been set to work in the hope that their knowledge of the stage or of movies might prove invigorating to opera. The results have varied wildly. Margaret Webster bridged the gap with a convincing *Don Carlo,* failed with an uninventive *Aida.* Alfred Lunt contrived an enchanting *Così fan tutte* and a hollow *Traviata;* Jean-Louis Barrault a respectable *Faust,* an unspeakable *Carmen.* The *Bohème* of Joseph L. Mankiewicz stands alone as uninviting. These at the Metropolitan. And I can recall a 1957 *Troyens* at Covent Garden with a share of its climaxes muffed by Sir John Gielgud's inability to get inside the music. At one great place, as Berlioz's rhythms rose sharply, inexorably in the orchestra, a host of helmeted goons shuffled aimlessly across the stage.

Which brings us to one of the more basic questions. How far should action mirror the music? How intimately ought they be connected? In opera, acting is only a part of the whole. In relating to the other components, it must never imitate, only throw fresh light. And so I do not contend that Sir John's soldiers were bound to execute a military spectacle. Their duty, that of the director, was to have aroused, through the music, an overpowering sense of urgency, inevitability, as Aeneas and his men left Carthage.

Such decisions are delicate in opera, where it is just as bad to duplicate as to ignore. We all remember the usual bit given to that gadfly, Annina, in the second act of *Rosenkavalier* when—with no dramatic reason beyond the three-quarter time in the orchestra—she waltzes around the stage. Sight must illumine, rather than approximate, sound. One element nurtures the other. For their symbiosis, a producer with an ear is needed.

The need would appear to have been filled by Tyrone Guthrie in his production of *Peter Grimes* at the Metropolitan. No single page of Britten's score passed him by, none of its tragedy or humor escaped him. The aural and atmospheric were as one. But the Guthrie visit, though important, was short-lived. He is back in the theater, probably thinking of his next operatic assignment in terms of three or four years from now.

An emerging replacement: Frank Corsaro, attached as producer to the New York City Opera. Corsaro's background is that of an actor. His knowledge of music is thorough, his ideas independent. Tradition, in the sense of routine, does not exist for him. His patterns grow from a fresh examination of the text, a look at its Freudian ledge.

Every move, in Corsaro's staging, is linked to the psyche. The connection may be explicit, revealed by the text; or if merely implied, hidden between the lines, then brought to light by the producer. This is theatrical reasoning that serves well in principle; but opera does not always accommodate. There are certain famous discrepancies, aching inconsistencies that a director would do better to overlook. The music takes care of them, the mood obscures them mercifully. Corsaro, in his earlier work, challenged these obscurities head-on. He has since relaxed, bringing to a recent *Pelléas et Mélisande* a less tightly woven, more open account of his skills.

A few qualified producers have spent most of their lives in the opera house—practical men of less than rarified talent who for the most part put on a good show. Two directors of this type thrive in New York: Tito Capobianco at the City Opera, and Nathaniel Merrill at the Metropolitan. Both are formidable in their way, efficient, productive, well organized, with Capobianco the more inventive. When it comes to evoking reflected baroque in *Giulio Cesare,* neo-Meyerbeerian pomp (*Don Rodrigo*), Hispanic pathology (*Bomarzo*), Capobianco's grasp of the offbeat leads him to success. I find his production of standard works less stimulating, rather lacking—even his celebrated mounting of *Manon*—in fantasy and charm.

He does, however, own a flair . . . knows how to deal out welcome surprises. Merrill and the scenic designer Robert O'Hearn, operating as a team, stick more doggedly to the conventional. No subscriber of goodwill might possibly protest the Christmas-window spangles of *Die Frau ohne Schatten,* marshmallow fillings of *L'Elisir d'Amore* and *Hänsel und Gretel,* civic splendors of *Aida,* even the monumental public bed of *Samson et Dalila,* all models of deference to well worn codes. Their *Meistersinger,* for the first two acts, shows more initiative in movement and decor. Less so a recent *Parsifal,* which falls back on symmetrical clichés.

Another team, more sophisticated, is made up of Giorgio De Lullo and Pier Luigi Pizzi, whose designs have been seen in New York in the Rome Opera's importation of *I Due Foscari.* Like his collaborator, Pizzi brings clarity and distinction to all he creates.

And a third combination brings Karajan in the role of producer with his trusted subordinate, Günther Schneider-Siemssen, as scenic artist for the *Ring.* Here the master's voice speaks out. We presume that Schneider-Siemssen listens. His work, as judged from the Metropolitan *Rheingold* and *Walküre,* is dutifully constructivist, in no real sense a departure from earlier concepts by Wieland Wagner.

Just as Zeffirelli turns me off with his frequent vulgarity, so does Jean-Pierre Ponnelle elate me with the grace, originality and wit of his stage direction *cum* theatrical design.

The points, brilliantly made, are never carried too far. Credit is given the perception and intelligence of the audience, ideas not hammered into the ground. The two productions by Ponnelle that I have seen so far have been comedies: *Così fan tutte* at Salzburg in 1969 and Haydn's rarity, *La fedeltà premiata,* played by an Italian company at Amsterdam in the following year. His humor is unerring, his taste impeccable, his resourcefulness as designer infinitely bright. There can be no doubt of his place at the top in seasons to come.

Worst scenery at the Metropolitan in recent years: Cecil Beaton's candy-box *Turandot,* outhouse *Traviata;* Attilio Colonello's *folies de grandeur* arrangement for *Luisa Miller,* in which a poor old soldier's Tyrolean cottage takes on the dimensions of an Alpine Hilton.

Best scenery: Boris Aronson's remarkable decor for Marvin David Levy's *Mourning Becomes Electra,* rich, organic, brooding, recalling the architectural power of a Joseph Urban. Note should be made as well of Michael Cacoyannis' superb staging of the same work. Both Aronson and Cacoyannis are among the elect of the American theater.

I conclude with a lament for *The Magic Flute,* most victimized scenically of operas. Perhaps it is the symbolic element that invites the laying on of hands, perhaps the aura of extravaganza. The latest assault came not long ago in Munich with Berlin-1927 type flats and tired projections by Josef Svoboda—parodies of an enigmatic masterpiece. If only the ideas had been new, no matter how far out; but the settings were gloomy and passé. Then there was a New York season not far back when the Lincoln Center houses offered a choice between Beni Montresor's Madison Avenue Egyptian and Chagall's all-out reminiscences of Vitebsk. In both cases, a part of the audience applauded scenery on an empty stage. Whenever that happens, something must be wrong.

6

THE MASSED FORCES

SINGERS, conductors, producers and designers work currently in a world market. Pay them enough and they'll
go anywhere for part of any season. Arrangements may have
to be made two or three years in advance, but everything can
turn out—and advantageously, for there is no question that
traveling stars build audience interest. In former years on the
Continent, guest artists would descend for a stay of weeks.
Today, with accelerated transport, they remain a single night.
Exclusive contracts to any one company as home base * have
vanished. Leading performers now spread themselves (and
their voices) thin, divide their schedules among many troupes.

Only the comprimarios (second-line singers) are on call by
the year, pillars of efficiency and morale. Yet they too may
have other goals, move onward. The fixed, quintessential
spirit of an opera house lies in what the Italians call *la massa*

* With the signal exception of the Hamburg Opera, under the direction of
Rolf Liebermann, which keeps a tightly knit ensemble, and of companies in
eastern Europe.

teatrale: orchestra, chorus, ballet . . . those anonymous forces that set the performance in motion, maintain a sense of continuity from one season to the next.

Around this permanent base, there are trends; and notable, over the past two decades, has been the improvement in sound of theater orchestras. Given the enormously complicated texture of all opera since Strauss, the players have had to stay alert, enlarge their skills. But not only the technique, the outlook has changed. Hard distinctions between symphonic and operatic organizations now tend to be blurred. The Vienna State Opera orchestra started the fusion years ago. These distinguished musicians, known in another incarnation as the Vienna Philharmonic, present regular concerts at the Musikvereinsaal, a lovely old hall not far from the opera house. Other great theaters, outstandingly La Scala, have followed; but the Scala players, though embracing the principle, order details differently. The start of their season is full-fledged symphonic—nothing but concerts—in the autumn. Then, when winter comes, opera takes over.

The complete breaking down of old barriers came not long ago with the Berlin Philharmonic, that guardian of concert tradition, recording Wagner's *Ring* with von Karajan and performing it under his direction in the new opera house at Salzburg. The legend of long standing about an alien technique, different orchestral approach and style for the playing of opera had been laid to rest.

Such a legend grew, in the first place, out of the specialized routine—memorized command of a comparatively small repertoire, speed in the application of knowledge—that is part of the theater. Opera men play almost by rote. If a singer should happen to skip, the orchestra skips with him. No questions, no time to think. The deed is done. Musicians in the pit need not count rests before coming in. They *know* the cues, the words, can spring to the rescue. Flexibility, even a kind of lawless prowl, remains the watchword. Symphonic playing in the classical mold is more literal, calls for measured serenity, Olympian reserve, polish of all details. A symphony orchestra has the benefit of many rehearsal hours; an operatic ensemble of comparatively few. Time for orchestral preparation in opera must be weighed against the other budgetary demands of action, lights, decor.

And so, toward the end of the last century, a particular type of musician developed in the pit: quick, rough and ready, precise on major arteries, slipshod in the byways. Above all, the man had to be so well experienced, so conversant with standard works that he could get by on minimum rehearsal. Most of these players forty or fifty years ago were drawn from a type now extinct: the "pit" musician, who also played in movie palaces, grand hotels, or vaudeville houses. With the advent of sound on the screen, the decline and death of vaudeville as a performing medium, an entire class of musicians was thrown out of work. Their way of life collapsed.

Out of this disaster came a new generation more limited in number, select in style, better able to cope with all types of technical problems. The younger breed of symphonic player would study operatic routine; and operatic musicians, now better educated in other forms, would keep their flexibility but add polish and style.

Yet although these men took on a technical ambivalence, passed it to their successors in the orchestras today, there can be no doubt that most rising professionals aim for a single goal: concert affiliation. Money determines the choice. Year-round contracts are now the rule for major symphonies; while only the Metropolitan, among major companies, can offer guaranteed annual employment. Pay at the big house is good, but the work is grueling: performance duty almost every night, rehearsals more often than not in the forenoon. Why, it may be asked, should first-class instrumentalists, employable anywhere, choose this grinding, semi-obscure life in the pit in preference to the relative ease and prestige of the concert platform? Put it down to that rage for opera which, once it enters the bloodstream, takes full possession. These players crave the presence of singers, lights, changes of scene. The penumbra of the orchestra pit is for them romantic. They feel a mystical attachment to colleagues in all walks of the company. This sensation, rooted more in the theater than in music, cannot be explained, only experienced. It is part of the spell on both sides of the footlights.

Theoretically there should be no difference today in tone and technique, given an equal amount of rehearsal hours, between the finest opera orchestra and a major symphony. The skills of the players are about the same. The modern opera man cares as much about polish as his symphonic colleague. Yet one built-in factor tips the scales. A large opera house will employ five or six principal conductors; the symphony orchestra only one. This means that the musicians of Cleveland, under the guidance of so exacting a maestro as the late George Szell had to mirror individually and collectively the character of their chief, render in full what he demanded. Szell's particular interest happened to be clarity, architectural line. Other qualities, subtle variations of color, rhythm, are tapped by the Philadelphians under Ormandy,

traditions established by Stokowski before him. Older color-
ists now gone (Beecham, Koussevitzky), great masters of
rhythm (Toscanini, Reiner) brought an unmistakable stamp
to their forces. They were field marshals.

Consider the changes imposed every night on an opera
orchestra. Except for those theaters with a general music
director, there is no controlling hand. Every conductor at the
Metropolitan shares the same authority *until he lifts the
stick* . . . and then the variations are amazing, a barometer
of the maestro in charge. The musicians are giving what he
wants; and sometimes what he wants is terrible. This rendering unto Caesar is no ironic act of sabotage, merely professional response. And so the orchestra of a first-class opera
house should never be judged at its worst, only its best. A
body of instrumentalists capable of giving Karajan what he
demands in *Das Rheingold,* going along with Böhm in *Die
Frau ohne Schatten,* with Bernstein in *Falstaff,* is a seriously
intentioned group.

Average skills in the Metropolitan orchestra approach those
of a first-class symphony, while the wind and string soloists
stand somewhat beyond. Their versatility is awesome. As
for individual character and personalities, the players have
changed radically over the years. Levels of pay, conditions
of dignity, general education order things differently in our
time. I have been told by a veteran of ancient days how
malign some of the men could be. Take the case of Alfred
Hertz, Wagnerian conductor at the house from 1902 to 1915.
Partially crippled, he would leave his cane at the far side of
the pit as he entered; and his enemies among the players
would seize the moment by greasing it—less humor than
torture. Such attitudes no longer exist. A working air pre-

vails, lightened by occasional puns. Some are not bad. . . .
When the Jugoslav conductor Berislav Klobučar substituted
for Karajan a few seasons back in several performances of
Die Walküre, the musicians—who admired his work—referred
to him cordially as Clubčar and to his wife as Loungečar. That
is today's aura.

The chorus, though vastly important in modern opera, cannot match the wealth of history, the diversity of means enjoyed by the orchestra. At its most eloquent—the "Wach' auf!"
chorale in the final scene of *Die Meistersinger,* the lament of
the Israelites in exile, "Va pensiero, sull' ali dorate" from
Nabucco, the great folk pages of *Boris Godounoff, Khovantschina*—the group is more than a musical or dramatic fill-in.
It represents, by power and point, a portion of humanity.
Indeed the passage from *Nabucco* was to become the cry of a
nation—uttered by exiles in Babylon but symbolizing, really,
the longing of Verdi's own countrymen for the unification of
Italy, languishing under Austrian rule. At first hearing, audiences identified with it to the point of frenzy. Such is the
power of the chorus to ignite.

This has not always been so. Massed voices in opera won
out only gradually . . . for emphasis at the beginning had
stopped with solo song. Evolution of the chorus as a dramatic
force took years, routed through Austria and France then
back to Italy, where the art was born. Standing on the
threshold of today's repertoire, I should choose Gluck as the
great choral path-breaker, *Orfeo ed Euridice* (Vienna, 1761)
as the landmark opera. The opening rites for Euridice with
their mood of collective grief, the overall fury of the scene
in Hades, the encompassing peace of the Elysian Fields are

all cast in a grand choral design. They are lengthy numbers, statuesque, of a dignity before which time itself seems respectfully to pause.

What new turn of mind could have taken hold of Gluck in his next work, *Alceste,* when he introduced a chorus so whispered, fleeting, swiftly paced—"Fuyons, nul espoir ne nous reste"—as to have brought a revolutionary sense of timing, of dramatic color into the opera house? Some brave impresario will hopefully revive *Alceste* (victim of too many darkly obscure productions), present it in the French classical style, introduce our younger opera-goers to the temple scene, not the least of whose wonders is the frightened, almost spastic reaction of the chorus to word by the Oracle that doom must overtake the King, unless another yield his life. Priests and courtiers exit hurriedly, leaving the Queen, Alceste, alone with her resolve to die. Their flight marks a thrilling moment, both of itself and as preparation for the crowning aria, "Divinités du Styx," that brings the scene to an end.

This revised version of *Alceste,* made by the composer for Paris in 1776, reached the boards when opera was no longer a youthful art. It ushered in the final quarter of the eighteenth century . . . yet even at that late date great scenes for chorus were to be found like nuggets rather than in prodigal amounts. Only with the Romantic tide in the early 1800's, a burst of superbly theatrical choruses, does one no longer have to seek top passages but is surrounded by them: the prisoners' hymn to freedom in *Fidelio;* the chorus of the hunt in *Der Freischütz;* the gathering of the cantons in *Guillaume Tell;* consecration of the swords in *Les Huguenots;* and, as a comic *tour,* the delightfully whispered gossip of the servants in *Don Pasquale.*

Then, from within the same century, comes that marvel of operatic togetherness, the capstone of solo, choral, dramatic, pictorial striving: the *concertato*. When the big moment arrives, principals, comprimarios, chorus and often ballet (for visual splendor) are assembled. One of the soloists intones an introductory phrase, called the *proposta*, kernel of all that is to follow. The other singers repeat this melody—its coloring and emphasis varied according to the characters they portray—and then, as a huge underpinning to the entire structure, the chorus emerges, voices of the principals soaring in descant above. Such passages, though outwardly static, are inwardly charged, bring almost an illusion of movement. When the *proposta*—a plea for mercy—is sounded by Amonasro in the triumphal scene of *Aida*,* taken by most of the other principals and chorus, challenged by the militant Ramfis and his priests; or when, following the Dance of the Hours in *La Gioconda*, Enzo Grimaldo launches his elegiac "Già ti veggo immota e smorta," the remaining soloists and chorus gathering the melody, piling climax on climax until the emotions of the listener are quite drained, we know—in the most powerful sense—what grand opera is about. Invariably the *concertato* represents the massed summit. From there to the end, as in the relatively intimate two final acts of *Aida*, the wonderfully concentrated closing scene of *Gioconda*, the camera eye contracts, the field of vision narrows.

Then there are the great separate numbers, less a show of drama than of mood, sculpture with voices: the Coronation Scene of *Boris Godounoff*, the Prologue to *Mefistofele*, Hymn to the Sun from *Iris*. Their aim is the projection of an epic

* The relative size of any operatic stage in Italy is computed not in terms of physical measurement but by the number of choristers and "supers" it can contain during the triumphal scene of *Aida*. Surprisingly, the largest playing area is said to be not that of La Scala but of the Teatro Massimo in Palermo.

sonority almost abstract. And in contrast come those scenes of personalized involvement, often of violence, demanding that every chorister, in addition to singing valiantly, be an actor. The Revolutionary Scene from that same *Boris,* the midsummer night's riot in *Die Meistersinger,* the storm and naval battle on which the curtain sweeps open in *Otello . . .* all of these call for communal impact, convincing individual strengths.

To this end today's choristers can qualify pictorially. They have improved in appearance, bearing and, on occasion (as in Tyrone Guthrie's staging of *Peter Grimes*), initiative. But unfortunately they sing no better now than formerly; in fact less well, a lapse we accept without murmur. Put it down to our tolerance of mediocre group singing, our acceptance of a Beethoven Ninth with luxury orchestra and student chorus. The concert halls, in this respect, may be faulted; they too often favor the amateur. Yet choral standards at the opera, though professional, are not much of an improvement. In place of the color, volume, all-out thrust of nineteenth-century repertoire, we are willing to settle for weak, sloppy sound.

What can be done? Amplification is not the answer, as in the New York City Opera's much praised (for my taste, excessively) performance of the Prologue to *Mefistofele.* The brazen voices miked from offstage may seem right for the planetary light show set up by the producer; but their quality—sullied and metallic—clashes with the nature of the music.

Neither can undernourishment—currently the case at the Metropolitan—get by. An auxiliary chorus does exist at the house for use in larger works, but the added resonance is not enough. With ever rising costs in personnel, it would appear that heroic size and volume may no longer be available, which leaves one alternative: the engagement of a resourceful chorus master. Energy and imagination at the top can do much, in any profession, to make up for insufficiencies below.

There is probably no element less vital to the performance of opera in our time than ballet which, in practice, can impede more than enhance. I write with an appreciation of opera's early indebtedness to dance, the influence of court pageantry, the quantity of movement in the operas of Gluck (one part ballet to two parts song), the famed position of dance in French opera of the last century; and to all of that I invoke a deferential *Requiescat.* Ballet as presented in most opera houses today is a milestone on an abandoned spur from the main road of dance. It is paid, in general, exorbitant attention.

Most opera ballets since the days of Gluck (in whose works the dances were indeed part of the drama) have been created as *divertissements:* ornaments hung around the central design, sometimes of diamonds, sometimes of paste. There are, of course, exceptions: the Royal Hunt and Storm of *Les Troyens,* the bacchanale of the Paris *Tannhäuser,* both looking forward to modern dance in totality of concept. But the greater portion of ballet's appeal in opera has derived less from artistry than sexual invitation. The big Paris house in the mid 1800's has been described by historians as antechamber to a seraglio—or, more appositely, a nest of obliging *rats de l'opéra,* available to wealthy subscribers who frequented the wings. Aesthetic considerations were minimal, new opera ballets beamed mainly at baldheaded row.* These

* No reference is here intended to the full-length, non-operatic ballets of the period, among them, *Giselle.*

numbers have come down to us on ice, without the sex or savor that once justified them, at least pragmatically. Not a lost art so much as one that barely existed.

Since the music remains, and get on with it we must, there is always room for a well-tailored corps in any first-class opera theater: trim, talented, adequately rehearsed. The problem lies not so much in assembling a dance group of sufficient size or skill as in spelling out its duties. The first-line company today goes overboard, engages many dancers, then may devise irritating, unnecessary stage bits to warrant the expenditure. Mixing them with the chorus in crowd scenes simply does not work. The choristers slouch, the dancers prance. It takes no great prescience on the part of an audience to tell them apart. Moreover hurling the dancers, as has sometimes been done at the Metropolitan, into the general action that follows a *divertissement* is to blur the structural line.

Needed: opera choreographers out of the ordinary (none in sight) who can suppress a cliché; enliven a scene with precision or—in the case of Gluck—with poetry; hew to the philosophy of ballet as an interpolated idea to be sharply thought, brilliantly performed. In such a frame of reference, the dances in *La Gioconda, Aida, Prince Igor, Faust, Manon* will glisten when stylishly done, heighten our enjoyment. They remain set numbers, and that should be the relation of almost all ballet to the parent opera: dazzling, incidental.

7

THE IMPRESARIOS

O F ALL the Italian words taken into the daily English of
our operatic life, *impresario* remains the most glamorous because it conveys the idea of power over all the other
exotic creatures in that half-world of the musical theater.
Maestri, prime donne, leading tenors, reigning stage director
—all absolute in their smaller kingdoms—must bend the knee
to the emperor who sets them up, moves them across the
boards. A few of the stars, on occasion, have rebelled against
his power . . . but in the end have streaked to earth.

Apart from the image of an autocrat in the trappings of
vested might, the word *impresario* also carries a more remote
and legendary connotation: the wandering *entrepreneur,* independent manager or showman touched with genius who
presents only the greatest of artists (discovered by him under
story-book circumstances) in attractions generally ahead of
their time. To complete the romantic picture, one sketches
in a gold-headed walking stick (the vestigial wand of Merlin).
Only surviving impresario in this tradition—with modifica-

tions tailored to our day—is Sol Hurok, intrepid developer of artists and of trends to which his managerial radar has committed him. Serge Diaghileff qualified in a broader sense, since he not only assembled great ballet troupes but personally determined their artistic worth. George Frideric Handel, if we scuttle chronology for the moment, was mightiest of the breed, with his grandiose seasons of London opera from 1719 to 1728. And I can imagine that Oscar Hammerstein in the first decade of our century must have been another wandering showman of quality, working magic at the Manhattan Opera House through performances by acclaimed singing-actors of a repertoire then dazzlingly new.

This adventurous element in the old-fashioned impresario grew out of his role as businessman yet near-creator, willing to face risks as well as rake in profits, take a chance on launching young singers and composers besides gaining from those already established. Domenico Barbaja, commissioning operas by Weber and Rossini, with the court theaters of both Vienna and Naples under his command; Bartolomeo Merelli, chief of La Scala, who encouraged the young Verdi and launched him with *Nabucco,* were managers in the classical mold. This kind of impresario leased his opera house from royal or ducal forces,* stood to profit handsomely if all went well but pay out if the season floundered. He was brave (climbing on to the back of the system in order to survive), perceptive (seeking out composers of talent) and often wily.

Toward the end of the 1800's, especially in the German-speaking states, this older type of impresario came to be replaced at the opera house by a team: the chief conductor,

---

* As far back as 1669, Pierre Perrin, librettist-impresario, successfully petitioned the King of France for the establishment of a private monopoly, the "Academy of Opera," later ceded by him to Jean-Baptiste Lully.

acting as general music director, and a titled court official who represented the monarch. If the nobleman, with final word in administrative matters, happened to be at odds with the conductor, it was the musician's head that fell.

Modern variants of this dual control exist, less stringently, in Italy by way of parliamentary committees. England works through councils. In present-day France the Minister of Culture personally wields the axe, selecting artistic chiefs and destroying them at will. And at the Metropolitan Opera in New York, a diversified board of directors chooses by vote the General Manager—or, as a wag I know would have it, the General Damager.

This post, in today's fragmented world, is unbelievably difficult and complex. The man who occupies it must not only be sensitive to artistic values, skilled at formulating administrative policy, grappling with problems of finance, but responsive to the moods of the community; and, in the case of the Metropolitan, this means the nation. No institution in our time can remain an island. Great universities have had to answer on principle to the towns in which they are contained. And the Metropolitan, as a company that solicits and receives contributions from every corner of the land, bears multiple responsibilities.

It has not always been so. During the long years of Giulio Gatti-Casazza (1908-35), attention was fixed—before the Crash—on board and subscribers alone. Efforts were made to satisfy as in a family. A man of exceptional culture, Gatti engaged the best performing artists, balanced his repertoire carefully, often inventively, even took stock—to a degree—of contemporary opera here and abroad. His interest in the

American potential, however, was limited. Those of us who recall his last seven or eight years of twilight glory remember a theater relatively unpretentious except for its roster of stars. The season was short, lasting about twenty-four weeks. Administratively, the staff was compact: General Manager, Assistant Manager, Treasurer, Musical Secretary. Labor relations, in our contemporary sense, hardly existed. The leading artists were well cared for, secondary singers (comprimarios) underpaid. Choristers had economic problems, dancers their own worries. Only orchestra men and stagehands ("grips") belonged to strong, protective unions.

Whatever the faults of this regime (basically the promotion of great stars at the expense of first-class supporting forces), its performances carried a certain brilliance, gave off solo authenticity. The box-office flourished until the Depression. Gatti's motto, to those outside the subscription circle, seemed to be a courteous version of "Take it or leave it." The public gratefully took it.

In appearance and mode, the man was aloof. His poise, his almost princely bearing, set him in the grand rather than flamboyant tradition. To the uninitiated he seemed a Keeper of the Flame; while among the informed there persisted rumors of offstage deals. Whatever their substance, this was a reign distinctive and generally rewarding. And in the background, until the onset of the Depression, stood Otto H. Kahn, chairman of the board, ready to assist in making good all deficits. This security disappeared with changing times. From 1931 onward the Metropolitan would have to step outside its subscription circle, appeal to the general public for help.

Herbert Witherspoon, chosen to succeed Gatti as General

Manager in 1935, died suddenly in the midst of preparations for his first season; and his replacement, Edward Johnson, stepped in to remain for fifteen years, creating an image at variance with the *gloire* that had gone before. He was accessible to everyone, tried without reserve to please. Totally eager, he tried perhaps too hard, set good will above discernment. His productions, in an era of shifting theatrical values, were generally archaic, his approach that of an amiable salesman rather than a major-league impresario. Yet before taking over the post, Johnson had rated as a tenor of quality, a good singing-actor, with musicianship and taste. Whatever his shortcomings in the job—lack of strength and vision—he never lost the idealism that had animated him as an artist; and he deserves in retrospect the gratitude of Metropolitan audiences for having developed the American singer as a commodity at a time when World War II cut off most European sources.

Like Gatti, Johnson worked with a small executive staff; but trends from outside the house were enlarging its scope, shaping its destiny, adding to its strains in a way that few opera-goers could have foreseen. Major broadcasts, successfully tested at a single performance in 1931, then put on with growing regularity from 1933, had already by the end of the Gatti regime made over the Metropolitan from a prestigious local into a national institution. The effect of these broadcasts, as they spilled into the Johnson era, was to transform both opera house and impresario, set them in a new relationship to board and subscribers, and—more importantly—to the listeners beyond. Untapped means for survival lay in that direction.

Simultaneously with the end of Gatti's reign came the

Metropolitan Opera Guild, a vital auxiliary founded in 1935 by Mrs. August Belmont. Its purpose was to raise funds with which to help the parent company; but in time the value of its methods matched the basic aim. The Guild grew into a medium for the exchange of ideas about opera; brought the Metropolitan—through lectures, publications, children's performances—in touch with the New York City schools and into libraries across the country; spread information about performance, history, aesthetics on a scale not previously attempted. It continues as a force in the Metropolitan today.

And still another development from outside affected the company in its crossover from Gatti to Johnson: comprimarios and chorus at last won an equitable wage through the chartering in 1937 of AGMA (the American Guild of Musical Artists), with such leading performers as Melchior and Tibbett among the founding members. The new union was formed for improvement of working conditions across the country, but sparked most notably a labor movement at the New York house that has grown ever more effective, involving all organized personnel.

When Rudolf Bing arrived on the scene (1950) as General Manager, he was expected to fit within this evolving picture. Actually he moved the frame outward on his own, transformed the Metropolitan from a comparatively limited operation to a big-business outfit. Soloists, chorus, ballet, orchestra, stagehands won employment for the first time on a year-round basis instead of the old seasonal arrangement. The administrative staff was radically increased, not only by more assistant managers but by numerous assistants to the assistants. They cost a good deal, as did, even more spectacularly, overwhelming new sets and costumes. In spite of generous gifts to make some of these lavish productions possible, the yearly deficit soared—especially after the move to Lincoln Center in 1966, which brought a threefold increase in maintenance. The modest, almost parochial organization of Gatti's day had become a giant. Executive routine, once centralized, was now widely dispersed. The office of artistic administration (contracts, schedules, lower-echelon casting), its powers and pretensions running like Ariadne's thread through the labyrinthine machinery of the troupe, would be first to expand. And then the technical staff—supervising the Lincoln Center plant, getting more than a score of big productions on stage every season at home and on tour—would edge nearer to the core of management. The subscription department, season extended to nearly forty weeks, its paperwork grown monumental; public relations, building prestige for the house not only as current showcase but cultural symbol; the development of a professional school and performing studio for gifted young artists—all would testify to changing times for opera. And the formation of a National Council—sponsoring annual auditions, linking Metropolitan agenda to regional groups—has added still another dimension.

Animating all this, controlling yet driven, sits the General Manager. Selection of repertoire, casting of topflight roles, engagement of singers, conductors, producers, scenic designers come his way at once. Though accountable to the board and indirectly to the public at large, he holds vast powers, can affect the careers of artists everywhere. He sets the tone, initiates the action. Behind the record of performances won or lost stand his personal tastes, nature, outlook. It is a situation not unlike, in greatly reduced implications, the presidency of the United States. The whole structure of the new

Metropolitan, despite its working diversity, may be characterized as one super pushbutton in the office of the impresario.
He is in effect commander-in-chief, with the last word but
also the ultimate, chilling responsibility.

Unlike Edward Johnson, Rudolf Bing never aimed, even
from the beginning, at pleasing everyone. He followed his
own beliefs with tenacity, held to his convictions, moved
without compromise—a course to be admired. The one flaw,
a matter of style, has lain in hypersensitivity to criticism,
acerb response to unfavorable reviews. Such devotion to one's
ideals, so strong a determination to serve them should, by
nature, allow no room for pique. Unilateral choice, lonely
mountain-top decision are the gambles taken by statesmen.
If the venture misfires, a classical silence should follow.

While hailing Bing's dedication to his credo, his refusal to
court an approving smile, I have often regretted the beliefs
themselves. Not all, to be sure. His love for Verdi, perhaps
the sunniest element in his makeup, has brought good performances to the master's better known operas, some striking
revivals among the unfamiliar.

Equally to his credit has been the improvement of the
Metropolitan's orchestra, a project begun under Johnson and
brought to fruition in the regime now passing. I have written
elsewhere of this group in detail: of its inequalities, shared
with all great operatic ensembles; of its amazingly high level
of solo skills. It ranks currently with the finest. Unfortunately, less may be said for—and indeed much against—the
present state of the chorus.

In staging, too, the situation has been transformed since
Bing's advent. Years before, under Gatti, much of the

scenery—and in particular the settings by Joseph Urban for *Pelléas, Turandot, Elektra,* the Grail Scene of *Parsifal*—had been beautiful, with lighting acceptable by standards of the day. A general deterioration, a sad air of shabbiness was to mark the visual side of the Johnson regime. And under both these impresarios, handicapped by a stage that was relatively unspacious, intractable, poorly equipped, the flow of the drama, its mechanical as distinguished from poetic pacing remained severely limited.

Using techniques long fashionable in central European houses and along Broadway but new to opera in this country, Bing transcended in part the famous handicaps of the old Metropolitan. New producers and designers were on hand to make the transition. Later, in Lincoln Center, came mountings on a more ambitious scale, prime commercial theater, sumptuously if unimaginatively done. What we had almost taken for granted with Gatti (primitive machinery) and with Johnson (spotty details, maculate groupings) was to disappear. In addition to hearing opera, we were seeing a show.

And as a showman, Bing's personality served him well. He was an original. The witty, often controversial statements; the ascetic, almost saintly head; the complete, unswervable individuality drew public interest if not always approval. Such qualities helped, never hindered . . . for they spread the picture of an impresario—strong, audacious—intent on remaking the repertoire in his image.

Yet for all the apparent surge, his choice of works was limited. The Metropolitan had become in essence an Italian opera house. Lip service was paid to the Russian repertoire by old-fashioned mountings of two Tchaikovsky operas. No

Moussorgsky * (a new *Boris,* it should be noted in fairness, was abandoned owing to labor difficulties), Rimsky, Borodin; no Prokofieff, Shostakovich. The *real* French repertoire, as distinguished from the inescapable *Faust* and *Carmen,* seemed not to exist. In 1969, the year of the Berlioz centenary, while Covent Garden was presenting *Les Troyens, Benvenuto Cellini,* and Sadler's Wells a staged version of *La Damnation de Faust,* not a note of this composer's music was heard. Of Spanish or Hispanic opera—Granados, Falla, Ginastera—nary a trace. Mozart, fortunately, came off in style with a particularly good production of *Così fan tutte;* Wagner, except for the Karajan *Ring,* less well.

Perhaps the noblest gesture made by Rudolf Bing, and the least appreciated, was his choice of a contemporary American opera with which to open the new house. The traditionalists were all rooting for *Aida* or *Turandot,* raising their voices publicly, whispering in spiteful little groups. That Samuel Barber's *Antony and Cleopatra* proved a failure (owing in part to top-heavy production) is beside the point. A risk was taken, a wager placed on new music for an important occasion. Bing's courage and in this case his sense of the appropriate have not, it seems to me, been bettered.

But how is one to explain his apparent disinterest in almost all other contemporary opera, excepting Barber's *Vanessa,* Marvin David Levy's *Mourning Becomes Electra* and, further back in time but more modern than either, *Wozzeck* and *Peter Grimes?* Much has been made of tyranny exerted by the box-office, the disinclination of any responsible impresario, haunted by specters of budget and deficit, to risk a financial failure, weaken his company at the roots. Yet the

* Except with settings out of the warehouse in Bing's early years.

New York City Opera, with a notable record of producing contemporary works, both domestic and foreign, has not only not closed its doors but spurred a growing audience.

My last regret has to do with the conventional look today of Bing's productions, their vein of aging Establishment. He took a giant step on arrival in New York, bringing stage practice in opera miraculously into the present, but the right foot has never since caught up with the enterprising left. There has been too little of the visually inventive, except in Boris Aronson's commanding sets for *Mourning Becomes Electra,* Chagall's odious but distinctive *Magic Flute,* Schneider-Siemssen's glorious *Rheingold;* not enough evidence of contemporary thought. I make no plea for strobes, mixed media, so quickly out of vogue, but have in mind more serious advances in lighting, movement, scenography from Bayreuth, Prague, Brussels and Commerce Street, New York, over the past twenty years. Only Karajan, as autonomous producer of the *Ring,* has tried to explore these breakthroughs, even if at times awkwardly. Others have conformed to standard design. Their productions have come out big, workable, smooth, with only the superb machinery relating to our era.

The reverse holds true for the Metropolitan's neighbor at Lincoln Center—the New York City Opera. The repertoire is adventurous, the productions modern . . . but Julius Rudel, the enterprising impresario, lacks Bing's charisma, brings less of passion than studied objectivity. An able conductor, he has combined the posts of music director and general manager, controlling all areas of the theater. Rudel chooses his operas adroitly and he casts strongly: Beverly Sills, Norman Treigle would be star singers in any house, and their colleagues do generally well. Orchestra is solid, chorus passable, settings and direction of good quality. At certain happy times, as in *Mefistofele, Pelléas, Bomarzo,* much of *Manon,* the performances glow. But too often one feels an aura of severity, longs for a group less contained, more open.

As for all-out exuberance, I mourn the disappearance of Alfredo Salmaggi—picture-book impresario, even to the gold-headed cane—and of his energetic sons from the operatic scene. The older Salmaggi produced popular-priced seasons at the Hippodrome, a mammoth old house * built for extravaganzas then given over to vaudeville, with an attractively tarnished air of its own; his sons continued at the Brooklyn Academy of Music. Their performances at best were wonderfully improvised, featuring the rocket that soars from stage to public without benefit of launching-pad. This feat—the triumph of the spontaneous—is not to be despised. It has, within bounds, marked some of the finest moments in Metropolitan history, recent and remote; and is, for my taste, the one ingredient lacking at the New York City Opera.

Most impresarios are developed after years of seasoning; but I know of one, Allen Sven Oxenberg, who sprang up full-grown in New York, there to flourish for fifteen years with the American Opera Society that was his creation. All works were offered in concert form, often with an orchestra no more than adequate. Semi-staging was employed, generally with skill. Such details mattered little to the public built by Oxenberg. The exciting thing was the repertoire—more catholic than one might have imagined, though leaning heavily on *bel canto*—coupled with Oxenberg's flair for casting the

* Demolished in 1939.

principal roles. He wasted small time, sympathy or money on comprimario parts. These were often poorly taken. But to his credit he presented several major singers, including Sutherland and Caballé, in their New York debuts and maintained his standards with others of prime quality, among them Callas. The project fell to earth for three disparate reasons: Oxenberg's principal guarantors (the deficit was always large) died or bowed out of public life; buffs eventually tired of concert opera; and the audience so carefully nurtured on demonstrations and cheering became in time a group of monsters, more intent on booing (fashionably, they thought) artists they did not like than acclaiming those they did. Music-lovers of sensitivity began to stay away. But the decline of the American Opera Society, its many evident flaws cannot ultimately weigh against the skill and imagination (so long as circumstances allowed) of Allen Sven Oxenberg. He was . . . is . . . relatively young for his length of professional service, with qualities—including arrogance—that mark the first-class entrepreneur. I have no doubt he will be heard from again.

Another creative impresario, more balanced than Oxenberg and substantially proven by time, is Kurt Herbert Adler, director for more than two decades of the San Francisco Opera. In choice of repertoire, importation of significant new singers, modernity of staging and production, he comes off perhaps best in this country's current list. Carol Fox, guiding spirit of the Chicago Lyric Opera, has moved gradually and with success from an orientation largely Italian to a more international point of view, while Lawrence Kelly, in a similar position with the Dallas Civic, travels for the most part in Miss Fox's former orbit. His repertoire is small, the performances of excellent quality. And in Baltimore,

Rosa Ponselle, the great Metropolitan diva of former years, has for many seasons been embarked on a second career as artistic director of the Civic Opera. Again we treat of a repertoire predominantly Italian and traditional; but within its confines Miss Ponselle puts her authority and wisdom to profitable use.

Here the pavement ends. I have not been in touch at first hand with the accomplishments of Glynn Ross and his company in Seattle, John Crosby in Sante Fe, Walter Herbert in San Diego and Houston, Victor Alessandro in San Antonio. They all have the reputation of creative men—with Crosby as an especially resourceful and brilliant mind. One striking name remains: the conductor-producer-impresario, Sarah Caldwell, versatile *in excelsis,* who has presented important premieres in Boston, great singers, good orchestral playing, imaginative stage direction. Her cross-country tour of a few seasons back failed financially as might have been expected with a brace of operas including—apart from *Tosca*—that Verdi caviar item, *Falstaff,* and Berg's *Lulu.* How could they have drawn in the boondocks? And still, as with Bing's choice of *Antony and Cleopatra* to open the new Metropolitan, her failure was a splendid one. Better to go under with honor than live eternally with *Traviata, Butterfly* and *Bohème.*

In England and on the Continent, the tradition of music director as artistic chief still holds as of this writing. Colin Davis at Covent Garden; Lorin Maazel at the Berlin Deutsche Oper; Herbert von Karajan (the rich man's Sarah Caldwell) in Salzburg. Time has not blunted the power of impresarios. If only more among them were to offer the music and related arts of our day!

8

THE ECHOES

I SETTLE under the gold on gold of the big house, look at the young standees intent behind the rail, link their eagerness to mine of earlier days, in an older theater. Much time has gone by; in spite of it, I am largely the same. Singing at its best thrills me always, especially in a new, commanding artist. It could not be otherwise. But how many performances of *Traviata* can one take? How many of *Faust,* even of *Meistersinger?*

Limited repertoire, shrunken outlook. These did not hold for every era. What a joy it must have been to live in the 1870's! The Vienna Opera had just opened its stately new building on the Ringstrasse. The Paris Opéra would soon be housed in the lavish quarters designed by Garnier. The Festspielhaus at Bayreuth would, before long, be giving its inaugural *Ring.* These theaters were symbols, outward marks of the new operatic splendor. But consider, more significantly, the great composers—Verdi, Wagner—still writing at the time, with masterpieces on the way; gifted youngsters—

Strauss, Massenet, Puccini—growing up, yet to be proved. Genius was in the air . . . not just in my retrospective thought. We know what these men created.

Where is that stimulation now? What to look for beyond the standard run? New singers alone cannot work the miracle through which opera stays alive. The need is for music written in our time.

Meanwhile, too much small talk about performance. I have never understood those fans who take every personality apart, dissect the voice, put the technique on the laboratory table, the phrasing under glass. The artist is their conversation piece, the art barely mentioned. I tire of all this, especially from the peripheral snobs who lord it. What they need is a romance not with performers but with opera itself—that glorious and passionate muse who outstrips all the divas held to be more important.

It is opera that I love, with the rage of vanished youth. How to keep her vibrant, ever in the vein? That indeed is today's problem. Seasonal subscriptions will run dry unless the renewal comes, fresh composers are found, new trends explored. Yes, even the pliant congregation will at last sink exhausted beside the long cocktail bar, champagne trickling unchecked along their trouser legs.

O General Damagers everywhere, give us something new!

INDEX